Hi,

Thank you for the purchase of this workbook. Doing simple drawings with pen and ink is a very relaxing and enjoyable hobby, and with this workbook, you will soon discover how easy it is as well .

The primary aim of this workbook is to teach you how to draw a pleasing wooded area with pen and ink. Drawing a wooded scene is one of my favorite drawing activity as it can be easily done from imagination anytime and is relatively easy to do once few simple rules are understood. Pen and Ink drawing medium is ideally suited to drawing foliage and indicating wood texture and in this workbook we will see how with few simple strokes, a drawing incorporating a wooded area can be easily done.

As you know, the term 'wooded setting' implies an incredible variety in terms of the feeling it evokes. It can be indicated by few big tall trees, or more of higher density of smaller trees, combination of shrubs with tall twigs etc. There really is no limit to the different approaches that can be used to create a wooded area setting.

In this workbook, I systematically cover different approaches to drawing a wooded area. My aim is to give you a 'tool kit' that can be used to convey different things and after learning these techniques, my hope is that not only will you be able to use them per illustrated instructions but also combine them in different ways to create your own setting.

Key is to experiment and explore different techniques presented here. This is the real fun with pen and ink drawing and especially with drawing a wooded setting. There are so many different ways in which you can 'evolve' your drawing and don't be afraid to do so. Let your creative instinct guide you and enjoy the creative process of discovering your own style and techniques.

In other volumes in this series, I cover drawing different elements of nature. These are not covered here and the focus is purely on drawing a wooded scene. I also cover how a wooded setting can be supplemented with other elements like a mountain, stones, rivers etc. but I encourage you to consult other volumes in the series to learn how to draw other elements. You can find more information on other volumes at **www.pendrawings.me/workbooks**

Happy Drawing,

Rahul Jain

www.pendrawings.me

Note on Pen and Paper:

So, what is a good pen for drawing?

Quite frankly, in the beginning, any good 'gel' pen will do, kind you will find in any local stationary shop. Choose one with fine tip (0.5mm wide or less) if you can find one. Gel pens for writing are often medium tip (0.7 mm) and their lines are often too thick to get good texture. As you progress in your journey and you desire better quality pens for drawing, you can check out my website and videos for more information.

www.pendrawings.me/penpaperchoices

Another great option is 'fine liners', which you can easily find with fine tip. One very popular brand is 'Pigma Micron', but to reiterate, any good fine point gel pen or marker/fine liner will do in the beginning.

I would suggest not using pencil. Most pencils don't give sufficiently dark lines that you need to create texture with lines alone. Permanence of pen lines also promote good observation and avoid 'draw-erase-draw' cycle that frustrates many beginners. Use of ordinary ball pen is also discouraged as their ink is not dark enough to enable proper texturing.

Most importantly, make sure that you don't get discouraged from trying activities in this workbook because you don't have a 'good quality' pen.

As for paper, in addition to this workbook, any normal paper like the one you use for normal printing will do. Avoid textured paper as this will interfere with flow of nib. Choose a smooth paper instead. There is again an incredible variety of paper available for drawing and you can find discussion on relative merits of these for pen and ink drawing at the above link.

Note on Proper Use of Pen for Drawing:

A key aspect of drawing with pen is to let your pen float on the paper with the nib/tip touching and releasing ink.

Never dig into the paper by pressing nib/tip in the paper.

Hold your pen lightly and release the tension in your hand. This will help you get the freedom of pen movement and lightness that contributes to good drawing practice.

A good quality gel pen and marker will provide a nice line with gentle touch on paper. If you find that you need to dig to get the ink out, then change the pen. 'Forcing' ink out of pen is never recommended. It will ruin drawing paper and create hard lines and ruin the drawing experience for you.

In the following pages, different pen strokes are illustrated that can be used to convey different textures. When attempting them, keep your hand supple and most importantly, keep it moving. The stroke shouldn't be done in a slow and deliberate manner, as this makes it rigid and un appealing. At the same time, don't rush through it. Find your speed and rhythm at which the pen line has a natural appeal. This takes time and practice and you will soon find yours.

Importance of Drawing Size and Pen Nib Size:

It is very important to understand that the level of detail you can put in your drawing depends on the size of your drawing and the nib width of your pen used for drawing. With a bigger drawing you get more area to work with and more details can be added when there is more drawing area available. Similarly, when drawing with a fine nib (0.4mm or less width), you can add finer details in less space compared to when using a wider nib. Choose appropriate drawing size based on the level of detail you wish to add in the drawing. I recommend using fine nib for most of you drawings as discussed in the beginning of the book.

When you come across a pen and ink drawing on paper or screen, it is important to understand that if might have been 'scaled down', especially if you feel that the lines/textures in the drawing as you are seeing are too fine to be rendered. Pen and Ink Drawings with finer details are usually drawn much bigger and then their scanned image is digitaily compressed/scaled down and used for printing purposes. Seeing such drawings will something make your feel discouraged as you may feel that finer details in such drawings are unattainable by you. But keep in mind that such drawings are usually drawn bigger and at that size, if you follow the techniques, you will be able to draw such details as well and on compression, your drawing will convey such feel as well.

Most of the drawings in this book are printed at their original drawing size. This is so that you can feel comfortable drawing them as you view them. Fine gel point pen (0.4mm) is used to draw them.

As you try the techniques and examples in this book, you may feel that they are not coming along well in the beginning. They will feel like just some scrambled line etc. But don't get discouraged. This is the nature of many of techniques presented here. In the beginning, there is no discernible outline and form when drawing a wooded scene with many techniques presented here, but as you proceed, it will start to emerge. Be persistent, and if initial drawing is not to your liking, then take a break and try again.

On Pen and Ink Drawing Style

If you had a chance to look at pen and ink drawings by different artists, I am sure one thing you would have noticed is the different 'style' of such drawings. The 'style' of a drawing is a loose term that generally refers to the way pen strokes are used to lay down tone and overall feeling the drawing evokes. In one aspect, Pen and Ink appears to be a very simple medium as a simple 'line' is used to lay down tone. But with this simplicity comes immense possibilities as there are limitless ways in which a 'line' can be drawn and used. At one end, there is 'Stippling' or 'Pointillism' where instead of line, multitudes of small dots are used to lay down tone. At the other end is use of bold brush strokes, usually used for drawing comics. In between, there are limitless ways in which lines can be drawn and used to create different feel for the drawing.

My 'style' and the one I present here is based on the use of simple pen lines to create what I call a 'pleasing' drawing. The size is often around 8 by 6 inches or less and is something that can be easily done in a small sketch book that can be easily carried around. What I recommend is to carry a pocket sketch book and pen with you and attempt these drawings in between your small breaks or whenever you feel like it. I don't aim for 'realism' in my drawings or instructions here. Such drawings are often done at much larger scale in a studio setting in slow deliberate manner. While you may eventually get there, my aim with the techniques and style presented here is to help you adopt pen and ink drawing as a relaxing and creative hobby that can be enjoyed anywhere. This means that my style and one presented here is aimed at use of simple pen lines at a small reasonable drawing size that can be attempted anywhere.

As you attempt the techniques and experiment with drawing with pen, you will develop your own style. Your drawings will look different than mine and that is completely fine. Indeed, your own 'style' might evolve over time as well. The key point is not to copy my drawings but instead to understand the key aspect of stroke as illustrated and then use it in your own manner.

If you feel frustrated, then take a break and try again. Persistent daily practice is key to improvement. Soon you will develop your own style and discover the joy of putting pen on paper and bringing to life the imagined or real landscape on a piece of paper.

Please note that all drawings and content in this workbook is my copy right and solely provided for your own personal use. It can't be used, resold or redistributed in any manner without my prior consent for any purpose other than personal use. As a pen and ink artist, my aim is to promote pen and ink drawing as a creative and relaxing hobby for all but please make sure that you obtain my consent before using the material in this workbook in any manner other than personal use.

For other workbooks in this series, please visit **www.pendrawings.me/workbooks**

Dedicated to all who seek to discover and express their creative side

Version 1

Do make use of all the space in this workbook and practice doing all the activities. As with mostly everything else, practice is the key to improving. If you don't like your initial attempt, then don't get discouraged and try again. Enjoy the process of discovering your creative side

Introduction:

At the most basic level, a wooded area consists of visible trunks and twigs surrounded by foliage. To provide perception of depth, we need to use different sizes and tones as elements further out are smaller in size with darker tones. Perception of depth is also established when trunks and twigs intersect and overlap in different ways. So, learning to draw a wooded setting consists of learning to draw:

1. intersecting trunks and twigs at different sizes.

2. Foliage with different tones to give perception of depth.

There are many ways of drawing and texturing above two points and we will cover few of these techniques in this book. A key consideration is the way foliage and trunks/twigs are combined in a drawing and based on how it is done in a drawing, the wooded areas drawn will have a different feel. This key aspect is illustrated in various techniques presented here.

Pen and Ink drawing medium differs from pencil in one fundamental aspect which is that a pen line can't be erased. Because of this, always start by laying out foreground elements first. This also establishes the space that is available to use for drawing background elements.

Relative order of elements is established when part of an element behind is not visible due to it being hidden by element in front. In addition, the background element receives less light and should be drawn with darker tone.

We start by looking at how to draw dense vines over the fence. This illustrates a very important concept of point 1 above, i.e. drawing the foreground elements first and then filling in the gap with additional elements. Here we will also learn how to draw a backdrop of stone wall and a wooden fence.

Same technique can also be used to draw a wooded area and is covered next.

Next various techniques to draw wooded areas are covered along with examples of how other elements can be added to quickly create pleasing landscapes.

Drawing a Wandering line:

The concept of a 'wandering line' is very important to understand as many elements in nature, especially, vines, twigs and even many trunks have this as their nature. Put simply, a wandering line is drawn with a 'loose hand' and gentle movement of pen to get a line with 'organic feel'. In contrast, a 'hard line' results when pen is held tight and drawn in slow deliberate manner.

Wandering
Line

Hard Line

To draw vines and twigs outline, draw tapering wandering lines as shown above

To establish the relative order, make the behind vine, discontinuous at the intersection point

Twigs intersecting and overlapping in interesting ways can be drawn the same way

Activity: Drawing a Wandering line and Overlapping Twigs:

To get a nice feel of overlapping twigs, some 'discontinuity' can be left when drawing a twig. This can then be used to indicate another twig going over that twig. This is necessary when drawing with pen as there is no 'erasing' of a line with pen. This approach is shown below. Practice drawing wandering lines and overlapping twigs in the space below and in your own drawing book.

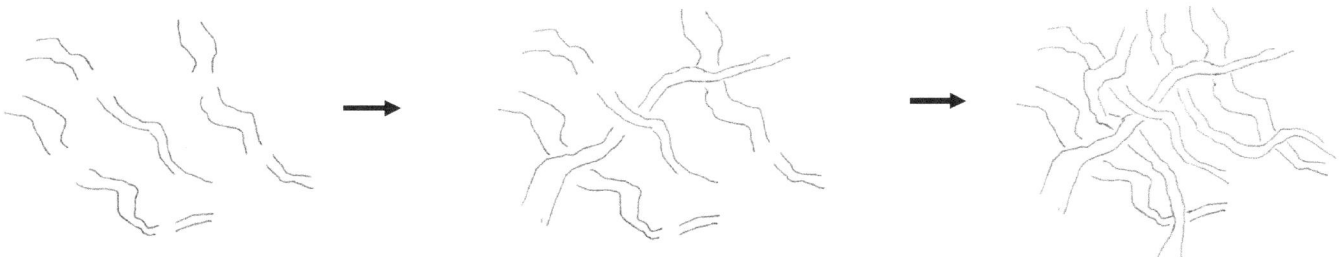

Leaving a discontinuity in a twig helps to achieve a nice feel of overlap which increases the drawing appeal. Practice drawing your own overlapping twigs in space below.

Drawing Vines over a Fence:

Start by drawing overlapping vines using wandering lines as discussed before. Keep the shape interesting with interesting overlaps and twists. Add more in the same manner.

Top shape like this indicates going over a fence

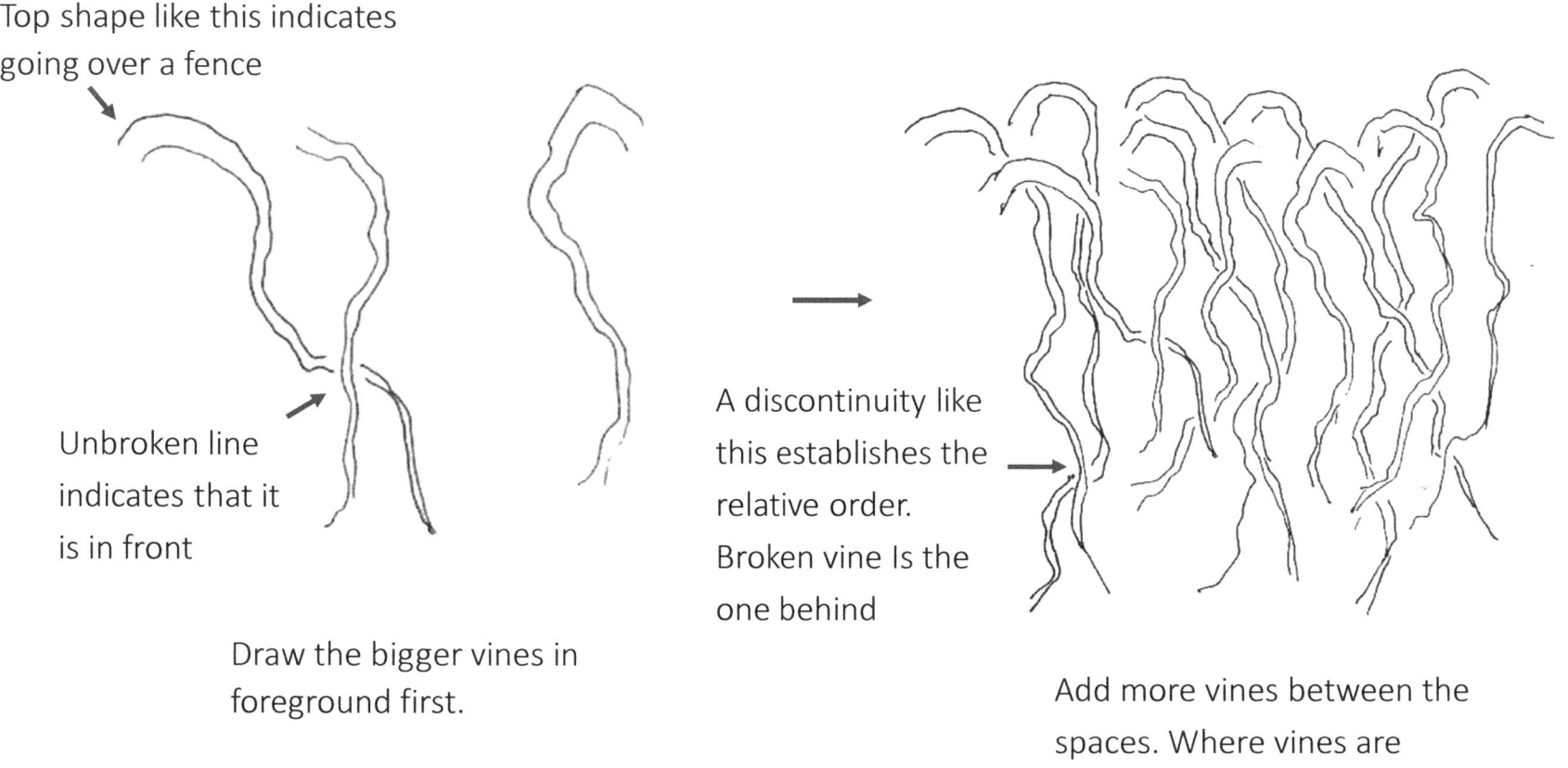

Unbroken line indicates that it is in front

Draw the bigger vines in foreground first.

A discontinuity like this establishes the relative order. Broken vine Is the one behind

Add more vines between the spaces. Where vines are intersecting, leave a discontinuity.

Drawing Vines over a Fence, Continued:

Use 2 tone technique (discussed next) to texture the vines. This simple technique adds a feeling of form/roundness to them.

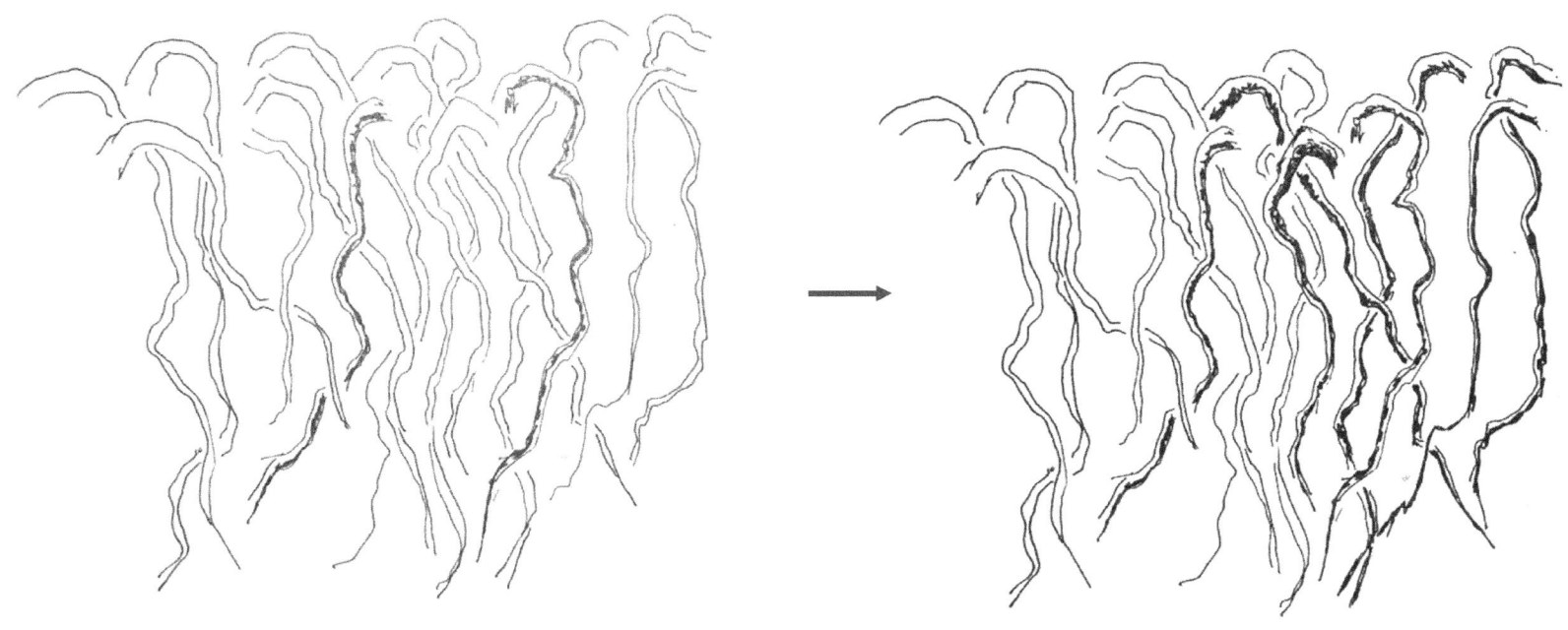

Darkening one end using 2 tone technique brings out their volume.

Do this for other vines as well. Now the volume and texturing of vines starts to give a nice feel to the drawing.

2 Tone Technique:

Light doesn't fall uniformly on any curved surface. .Area that is facing the light source (usually Sun for landscapes) is lit brightest while the area that is away from the light source is darkest. By indicating such tonal variation for a curved surface, the rounded form of the object is perceived.

For smaller sized drawings, usually 3 tones of varying intensity (light, middle and dark tone) are enough to bring out the form as shown below. But as the size of object reduces, such 3 tones can't be properly textured and in this case, 2 tone technique is used. In 2 one technique, only 2 tones (light and dark) are used (middle tone is omitted). By darkening one side of the outline in a zagged manner to add dark tone, perception of volume is achieved as shown below.

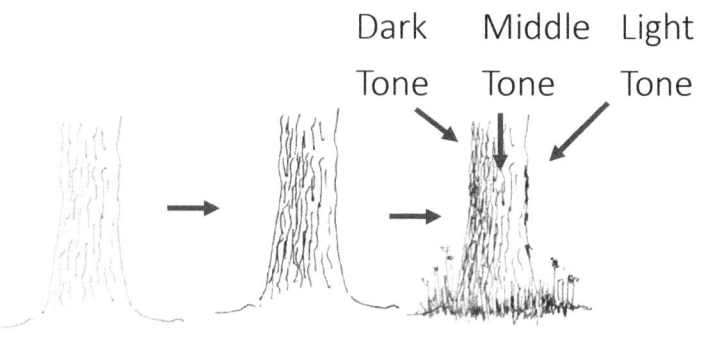

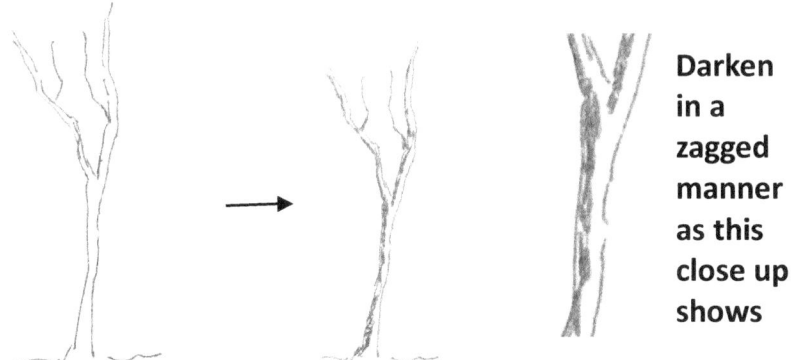

Darken in a zagged manner as this close up shows

When the size of object is relative bigger, pen strokes can be used to impart 3 tones to bring out the form.

At this size, 3 tones can't be imparted. In this case, one end of the outline is darkened in a zagged manner to make it darker. This brings out the form as there is tonal variation from light to dark.

2 Tone Technique, Continued:

Here are some more examples of 2 tone technique. Small twigs, far away trunks, thin branches etc. are usually done using this technique.

As the size further reduces, solid tapered dark is usually used. Tonal study below illustrates these points.

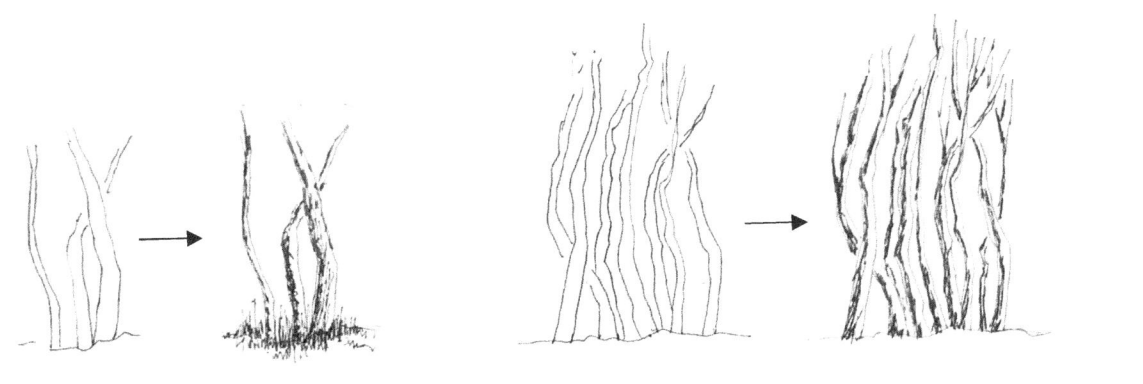

2 tone technique used to draw tall twigs, vines, thin trunks etc.

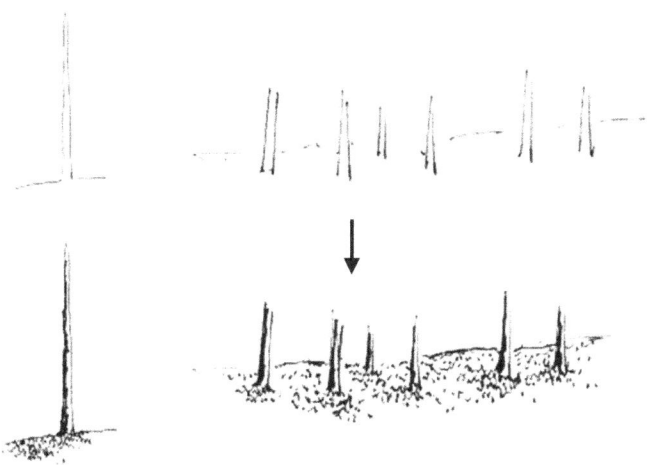

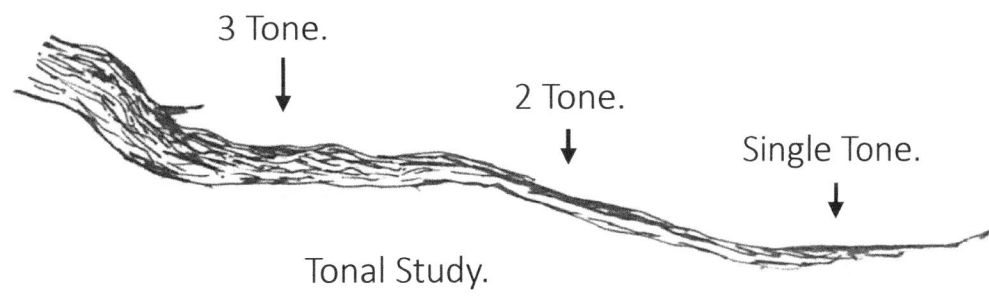

Tonal Study.

3 tones (dark, middle and light) are used when drawing area allows it. As it becomes less, 2 tone (dark and light) is used and finally dark tone is used.

2 Tone Technique, Continued:

In addition, other outline can also be darkened in 2 tone technique. Darken it less than the other side as shown below.

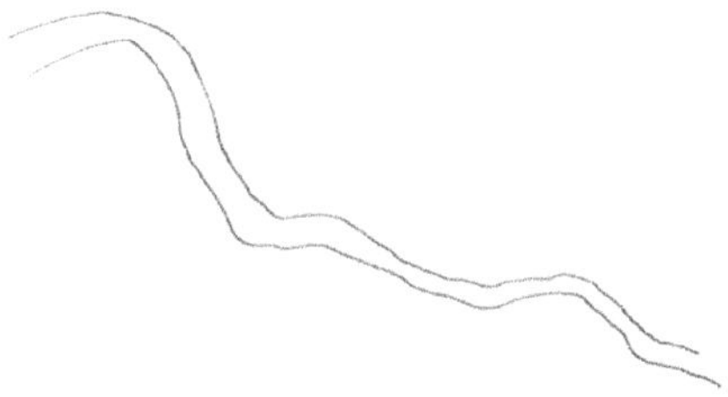

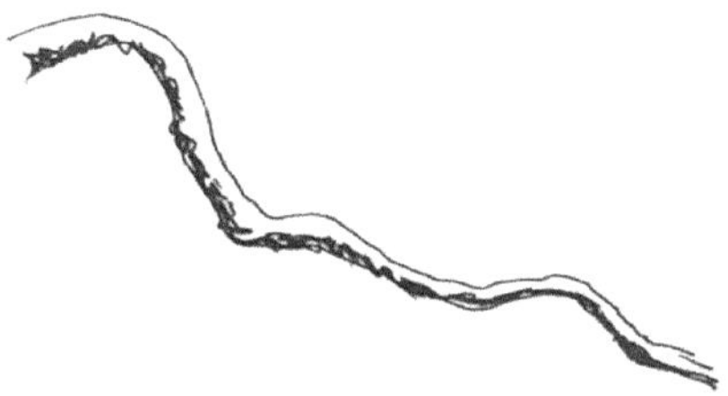

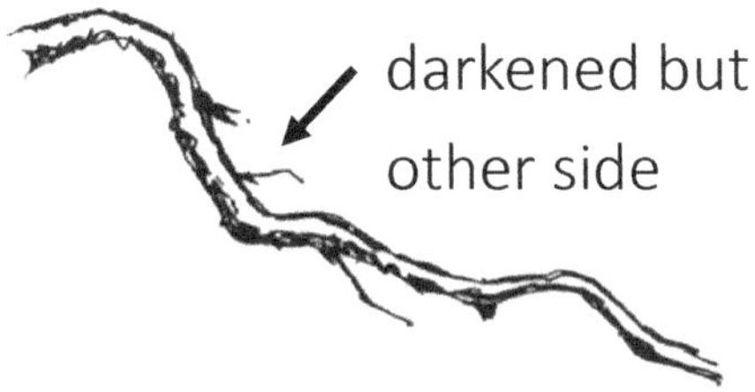

Other outline can be also darkened but less than other side

Start by drawing the outline as before

Add dark tone to one side, almost 1/3, as shown above

Other outline can also be made slightly darker. The sliver of white in the center is most important as this indicates highlight and brings out the rounded form.

Direction of Light (Sun)

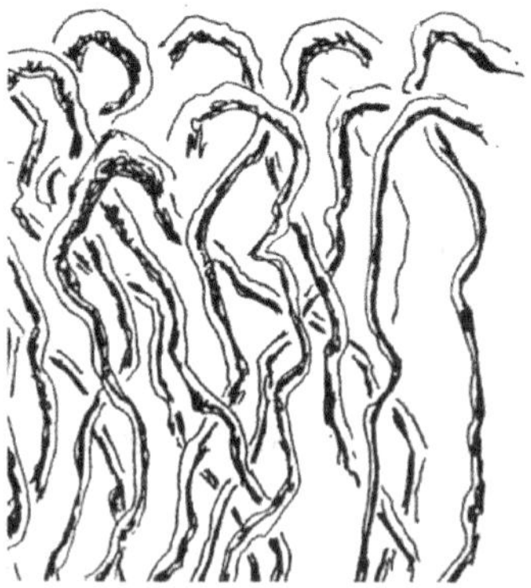

Keep the darkening consistent. Twigs going left and right side will be darkened differently based on the direction of light source as this drawing indicates.

Activity: Using 2 Tone Technique:

Add texturing to the following twigs using 2 tone technique as discussed earlier. Add 2 tones to the drawing you did in previous activity.

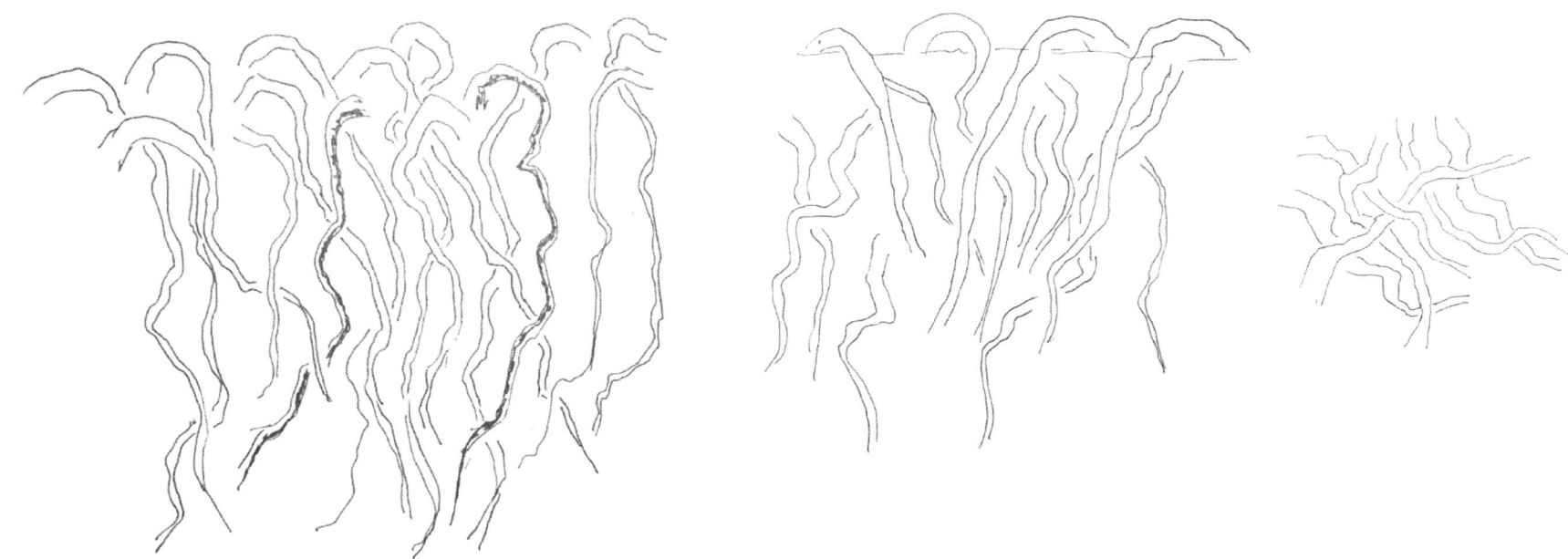

Drawing Vines Over a Fence, Continued:

Add more vines in the space between to give it more density to your liking. Texture them using the same 2 tone technique and use solid tapered dark for the end. This completes drawing of vines. Next we look at drawing a backdrop for it.

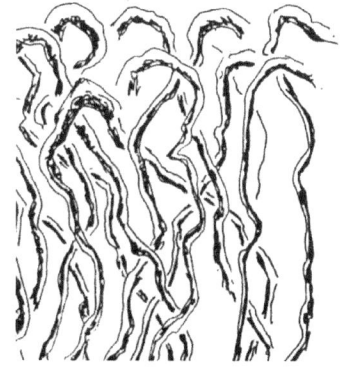

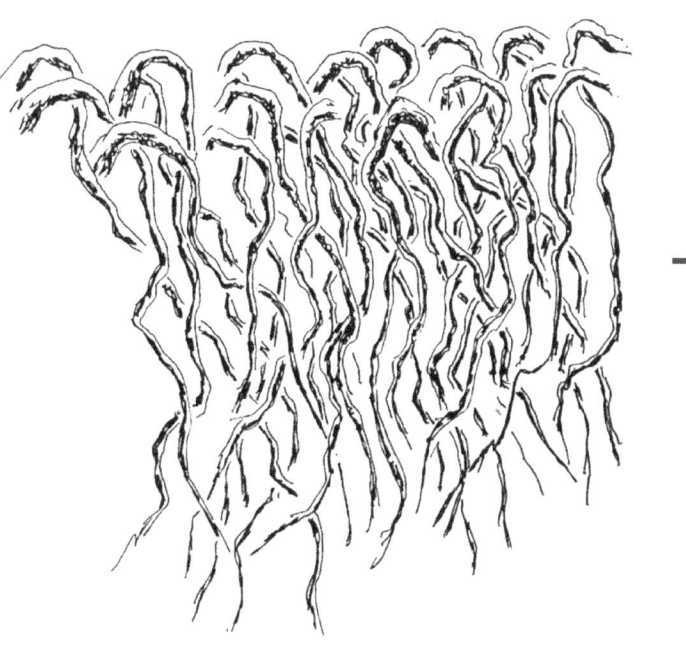

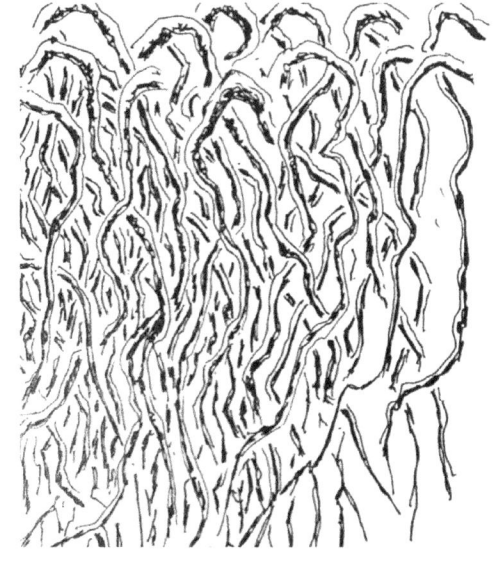

Study how by using random overlapping of vines, perception of depth is achieved. Strive for this in your drawing. Avoid any repetition and pattern.

Continue by adding more vines in the space between and texturing them using 2 tone technique.

Higher volume of vines/twigs usually gives a pleasing feel. Experiment to see what you prefer.

For more information visit www.pendrawings.me/getstarted

Drawing Vines over a Fence, Continued:

Here we will learn how to draw a backdrop of stone/brick wall for the vines/twigs. A nice backdrop adds great visual interest to the drawing.

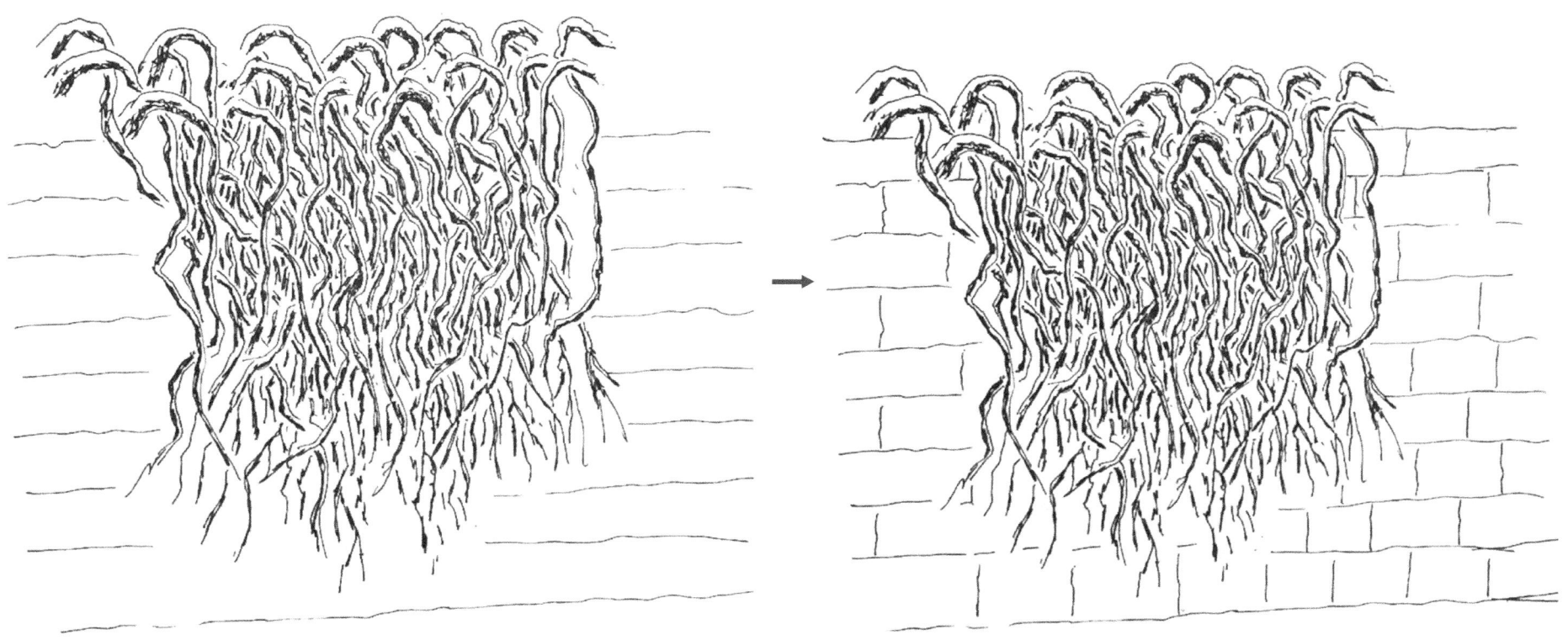

Start by drawing horizontal lines to represent bricks.

Add staggered vertical lines to represent individual bricks as shown above.

Drawing Vines over a Fence, continued:

Drawing a backdrop of stone/brick wall adds great visual interest and can be done as shown below.

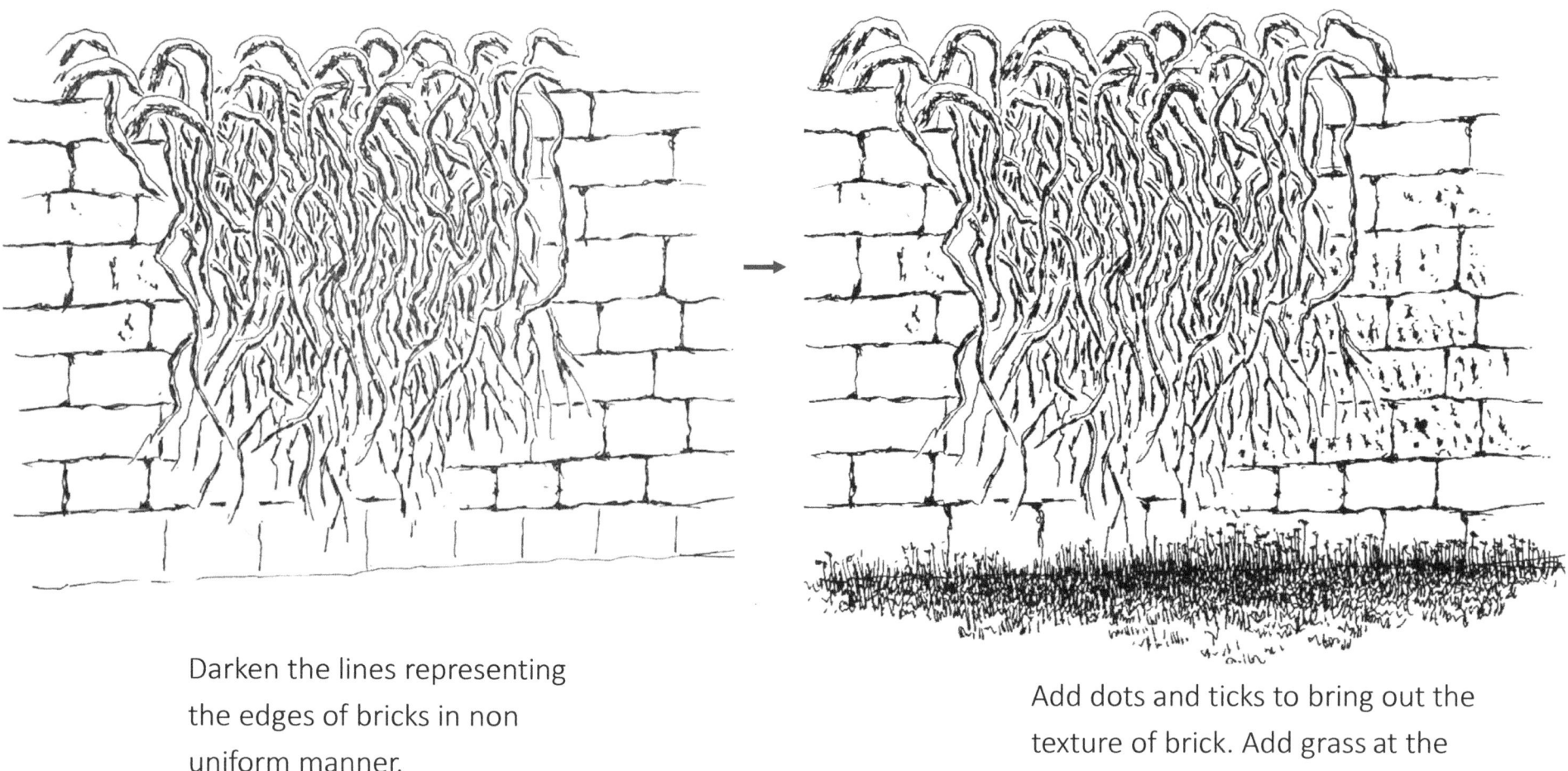

Darken the lines representing the edges of bricks in non uniform manner.

Add dots and ticks to bring out the texture of brick. Add grass at the bottom to ground it.

Drawing Vines over a Fence, Completed:

Add Sky to finish the drawing. Adding grass is discussed at the end of the workbook.

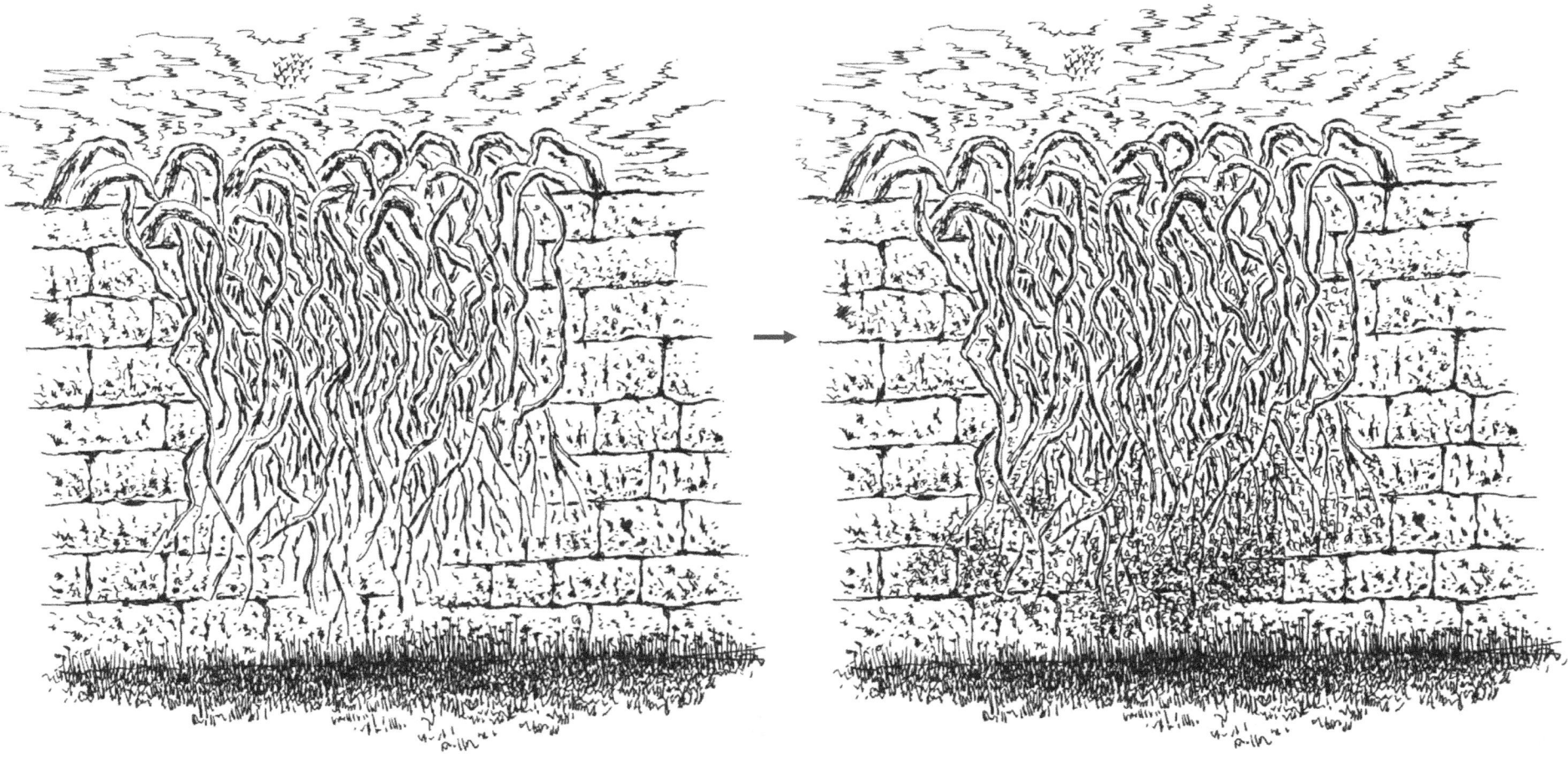

Texture other bricks in a similar manner. Add Sky to finish. As there is no foliage, it gives a feel of winter setting.

Some foliage/leaves can be added at the end to get a different feel.

Choosing Density of Foliage:

One of the main design decisions is choosing relative density of foliage vs non foliage elements (twigs/trunks). If more foliage is used, then it gives a different feel compared to drawings where twigs/trunks are given prominence. This is shown below. By using right level of foliage in your composition, you can get the right feel for your drawing.

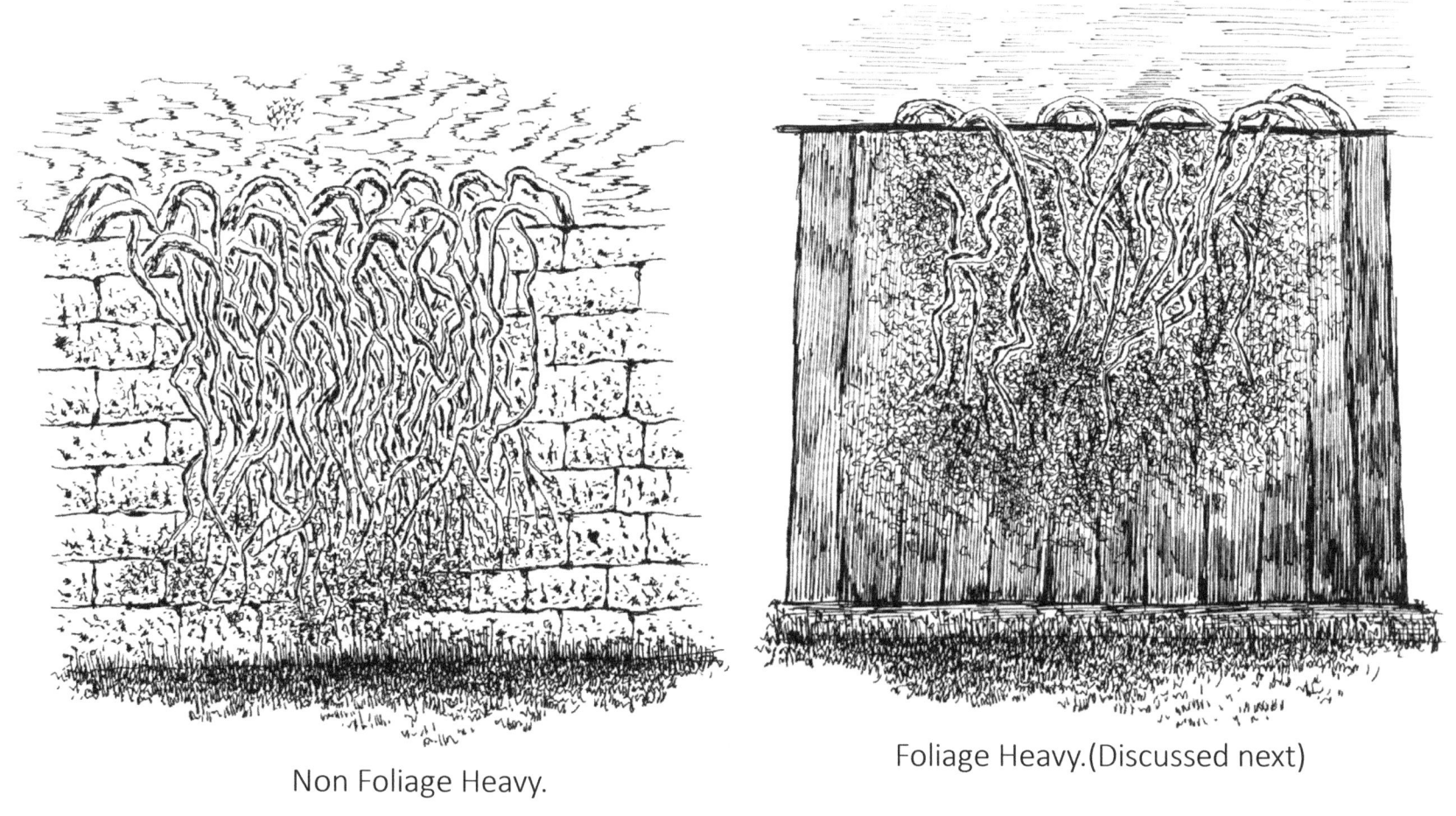

Non Foliage Heavy.

Foliage Heavy.(Discussed next)

For a foliage heavy feel, after some initial twigs/trunks are added, add more foliage in the space between. This is illustrated next.

Drawing Vines over a Fence with Dense Foliage:

Here we look at how to do similar composition as last one but instead with more use of foliage. To give more feel of foliage, after some foreground main vines are added, the space is filled with foliage to give more prominence to it.

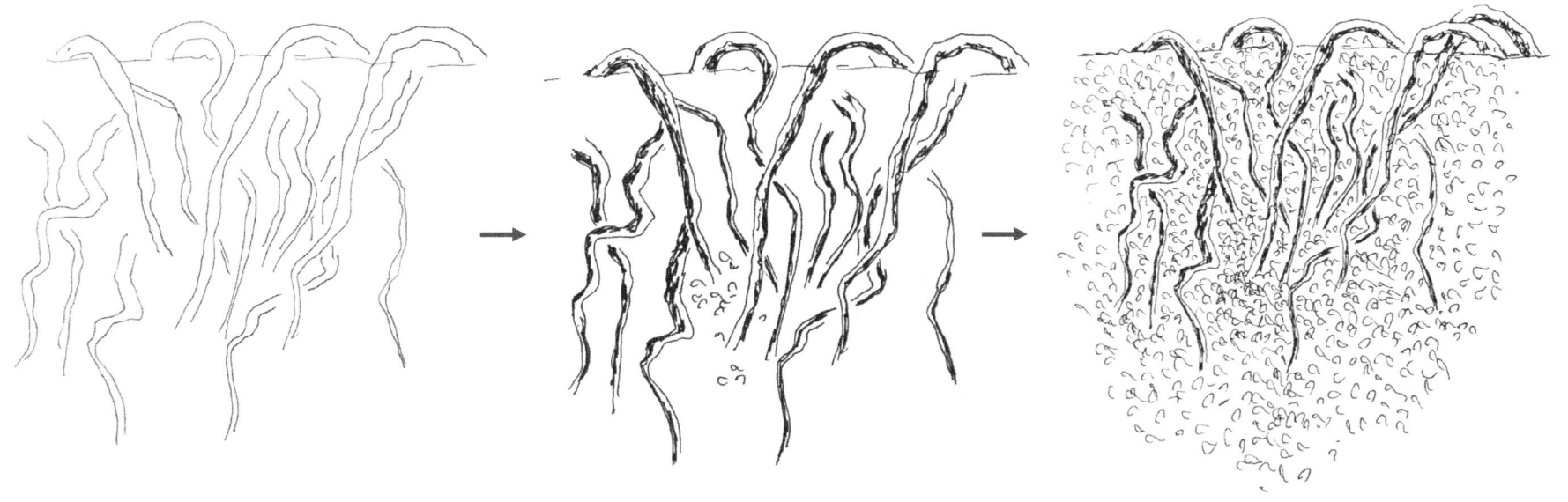

Start by drawing and texturing the foreground vines as before.

Instead of adding more density of vines, draw foliage using leaf stroke as discussed in next page.

Drawing Foliage:

Foliage can be drawn using many different strokes and some of them are discussed in this book. Most important thing is to draw these strokes in a random manner. Drawing foliage is discussed in more detail in other volumes in this series. You can get more information about other volumes at www.pendrawings.me/workbooks.

Basic 'leaf' stroke:
Use open loops like these in different directions to indicate foliage

Following are 2 other simple Foliage Strokes:

Scribble Stroke   Loopy Stroke

Ticks marks and swirls like these can be used as well

In fact, Any stroke with open curvy feel can be used to draw foliage. Following illustrates some of these strokes. As you get more experienced, you can draw such strokes on the fly and create more pleasing feel of foliage instead of using a specific stroke.

Avoid any pattern by using the stroke in different sizes and different orientations

No Pattern

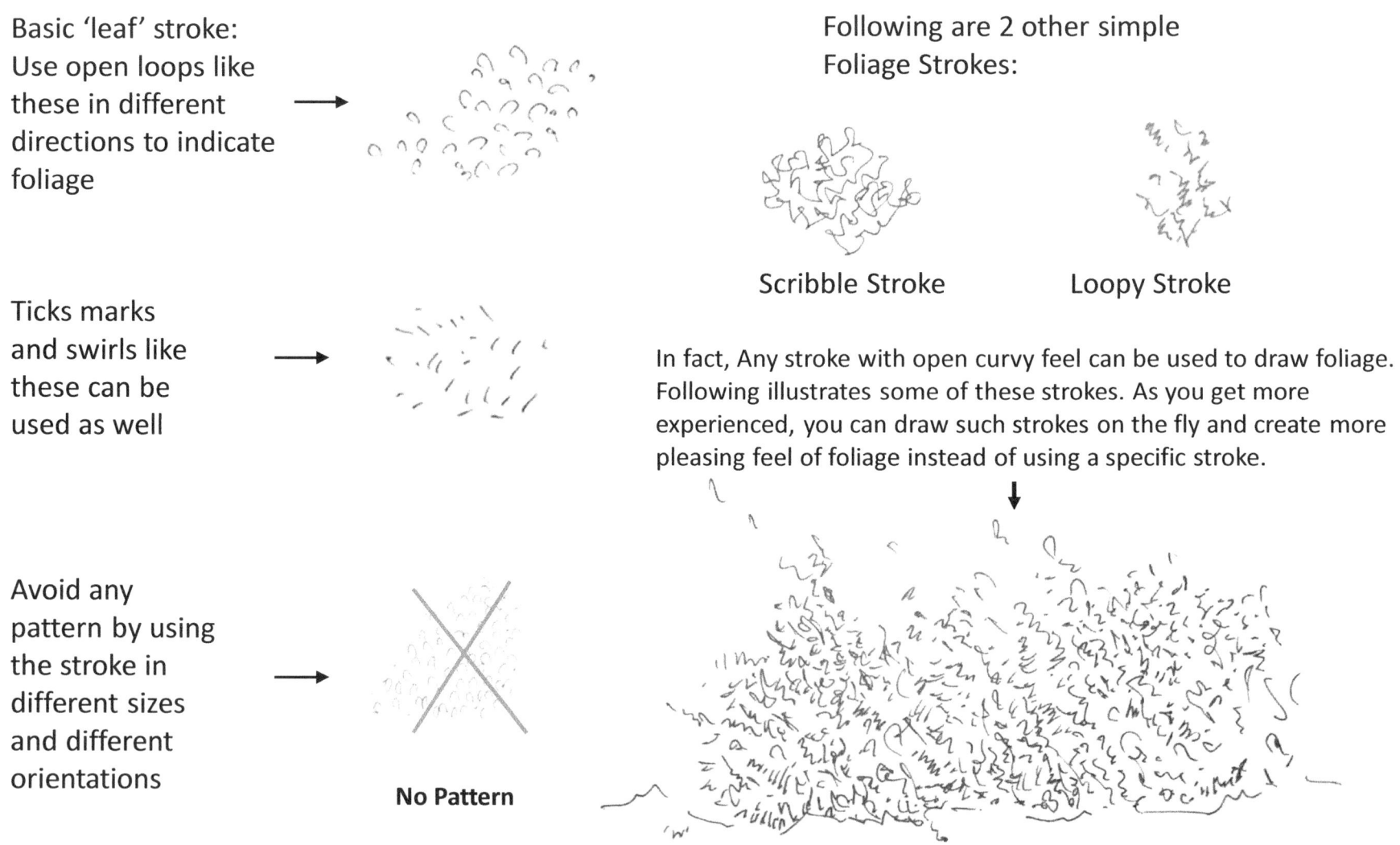

For more information visit www.pendrawings.me/getstarted

Activity: Practice Drawing Foliage:

Practice drawing the following foliage strokes.

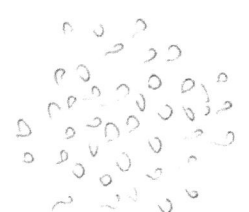 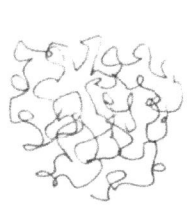 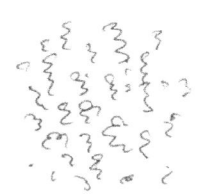

Importance of Tonal Variation in Foliage:

Tonal variation (different levels of light and dark) is a fundamental aspect of drawing. Perception of depth is established only when there is a tonal variation, especially in objects with curved irregular surfaces. For a regularly curved surface, like a cylinder, the tonal variation is gradual and follows the curve of the surface. For an irregular surface like a foliage, tonal variation needs to be drawn in an irregular manner for the perception of depth to come out.

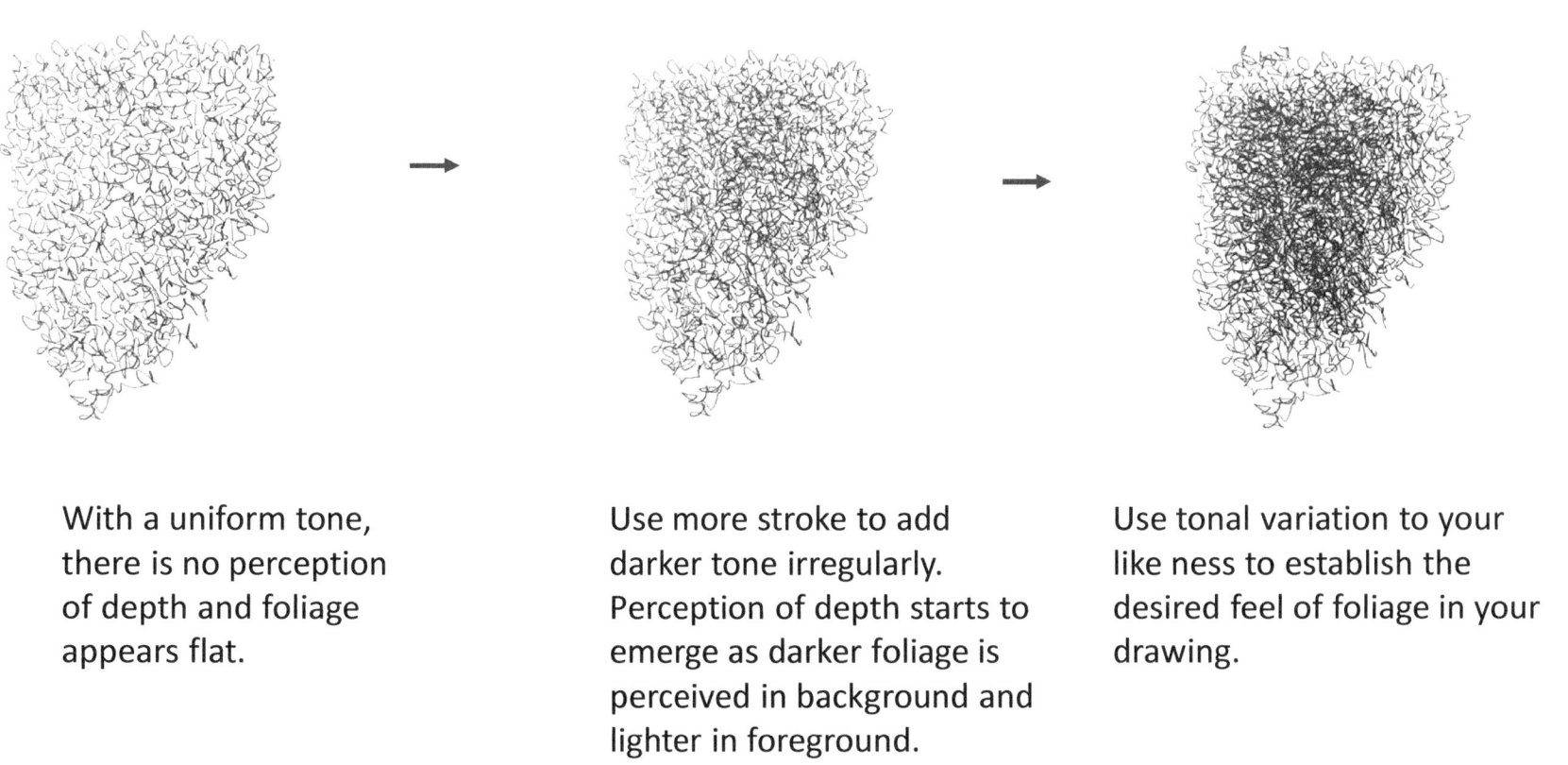

With a uniform tone, there is no perception of depth and foliage appears flat.

Use more stroke to add darker tone irregularly. Perception of depth starts to emerge as darker foliage is perceived in background and lighter in foreground.

Use tonal variation to your like ness to establish the desired feel of foliage in your drawing.

Drawing Vines over a Fence with Dense Foliage, Continued:

Draw the density of foliage to your liking. Vary the density of foliage to bring out volume and depth.

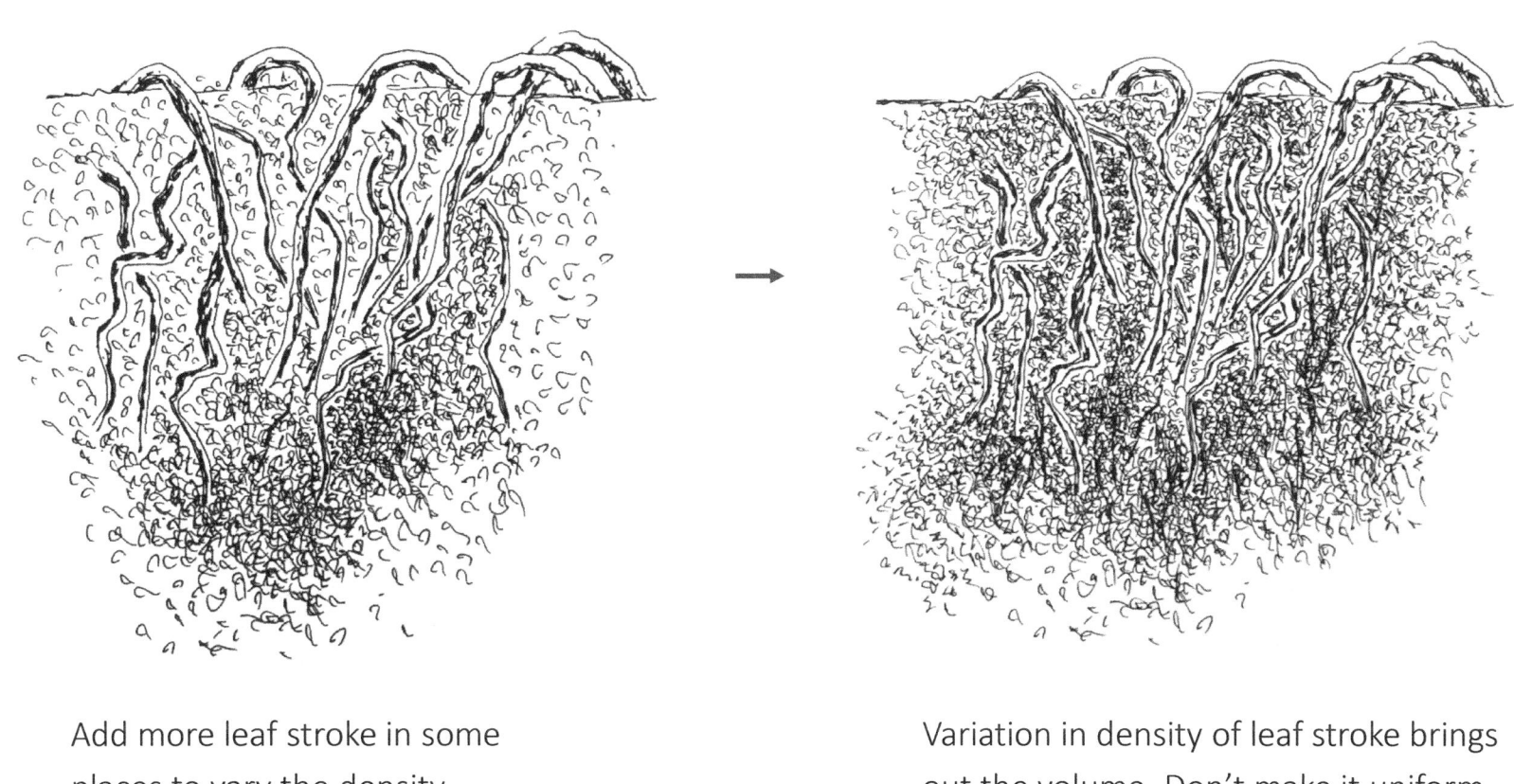

Add more leaf stroke in some places to vary the density.

Variation in density of leaf stroke brings out the volume. Don't make it uniform.

Steps for drawing foliage and importance of tonal variation in foliage depiction is discussed in detail in volume 1&2 of the series. Pl. visit www.pendrawings.me/workbooks for more information.

Drawing Vines over a fence with Dense Foliage, Completed:

Here a wooden fence is drawn as the backdrop to the vines.

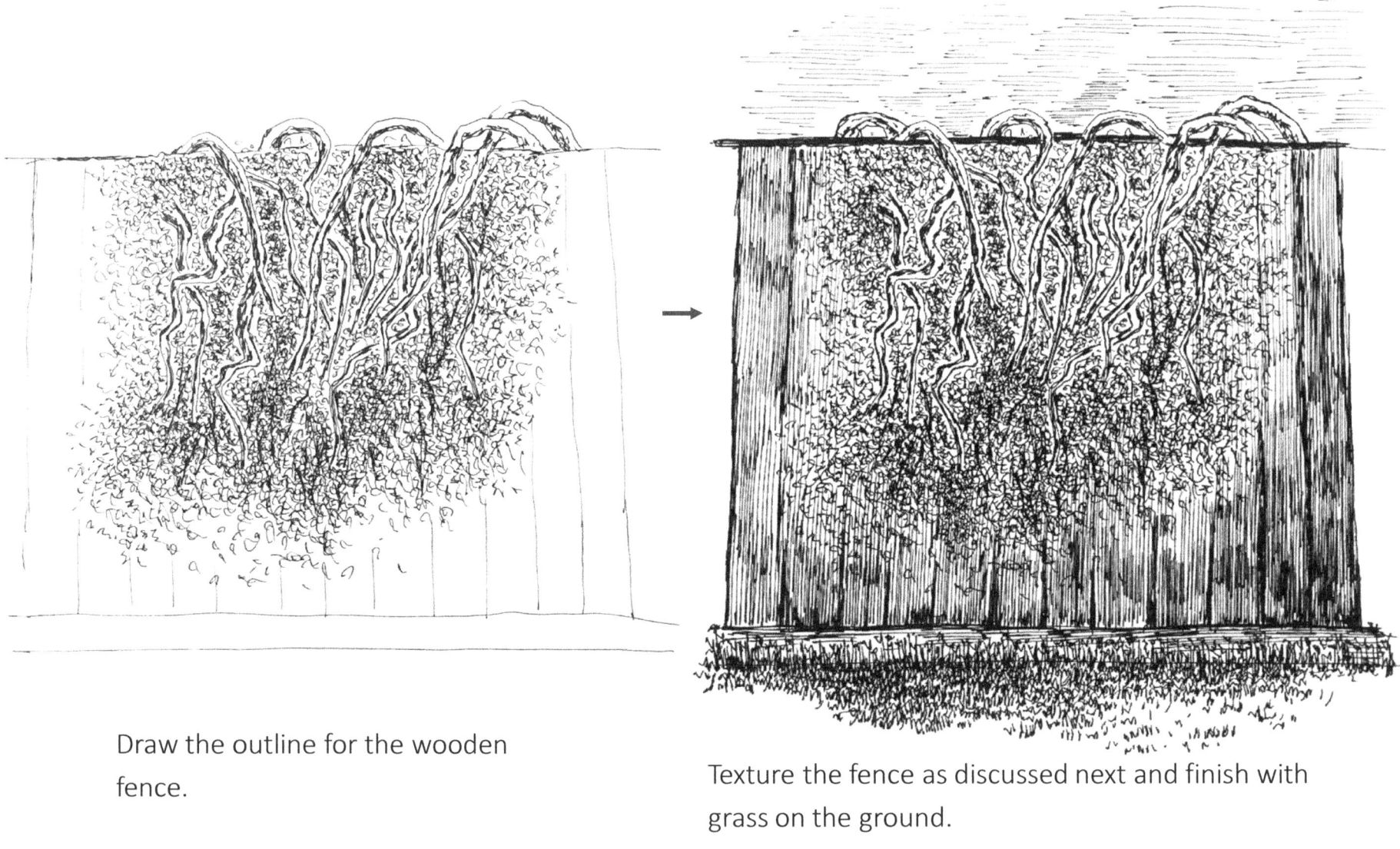

Draw the outline for the wooden fence.

Texture the fence as discussed next and finish with grass on the ground.

Drawing A Wooden Fence:

Following steps can be used to draw a wooden fence. This is discussed further in vol. 4 of the series. You can find more details on other volumes at www.pendrawings.me/workbooks.

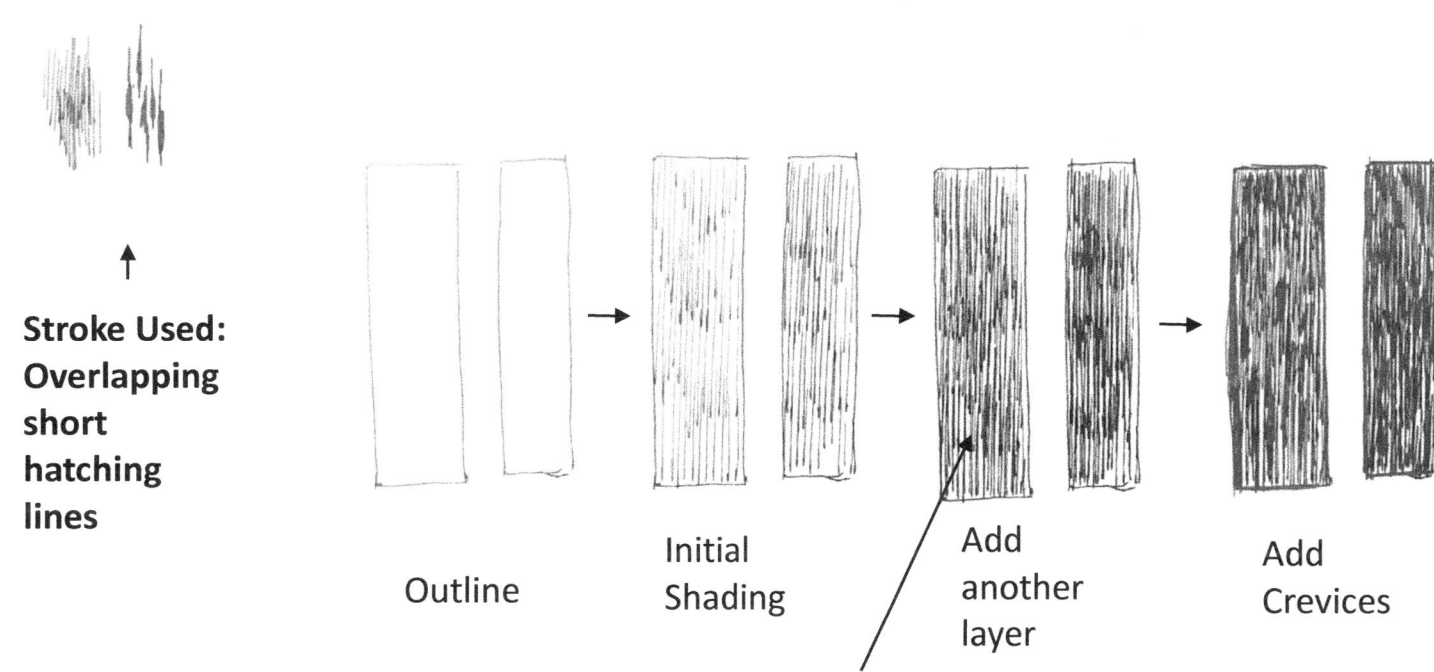

Stroke Used: Overlapping short hatching lines

Outline → Initial Shading → Add another layer → Add Crevices

Overlapping lines create darker areas which creates feel of wooden texture

Importance of Contrast:

In the absence of colors, contrast of tones between different elements in a pen and ink drawing is very important. This is the main way in which our eyes can distinguish between different elements and make sense of the drawing. This is especially important between two adjacent elements. In the following drawing, the difference in tone between wooden fence and the vines/foliage in front makes the drawing appealing. If they were to be textured to the same level of darkness, the drawing would loose its appeal and viewer's eyes would struggle to find focal points. Make sure you have such contrasts in your drawings.

Overall tone of wooden fence is darker than vine/foliage to provide contrast between them and help our eyes distinguish between them.

Level of Detail:

As mentioned in the beginning, level of detail that can be added to a drawing is usually dependent on the size of the drawing and nib width of your drawing pen. Put simply, with more space, more details can be added using finer nib. But keep in mind that level of detail you may want to use in your drawing is also dependent on the feel you want to evoke in your drawing. For a feel of quick, fluid sketch, higher level of detail is not needed. Generally, higher level of detail gives a feel of more deliberate drawing attempt to the finished work. Following is an example of my drawing drawn at 8 by 10 inches using .44 mm Uni-ball gel pen.

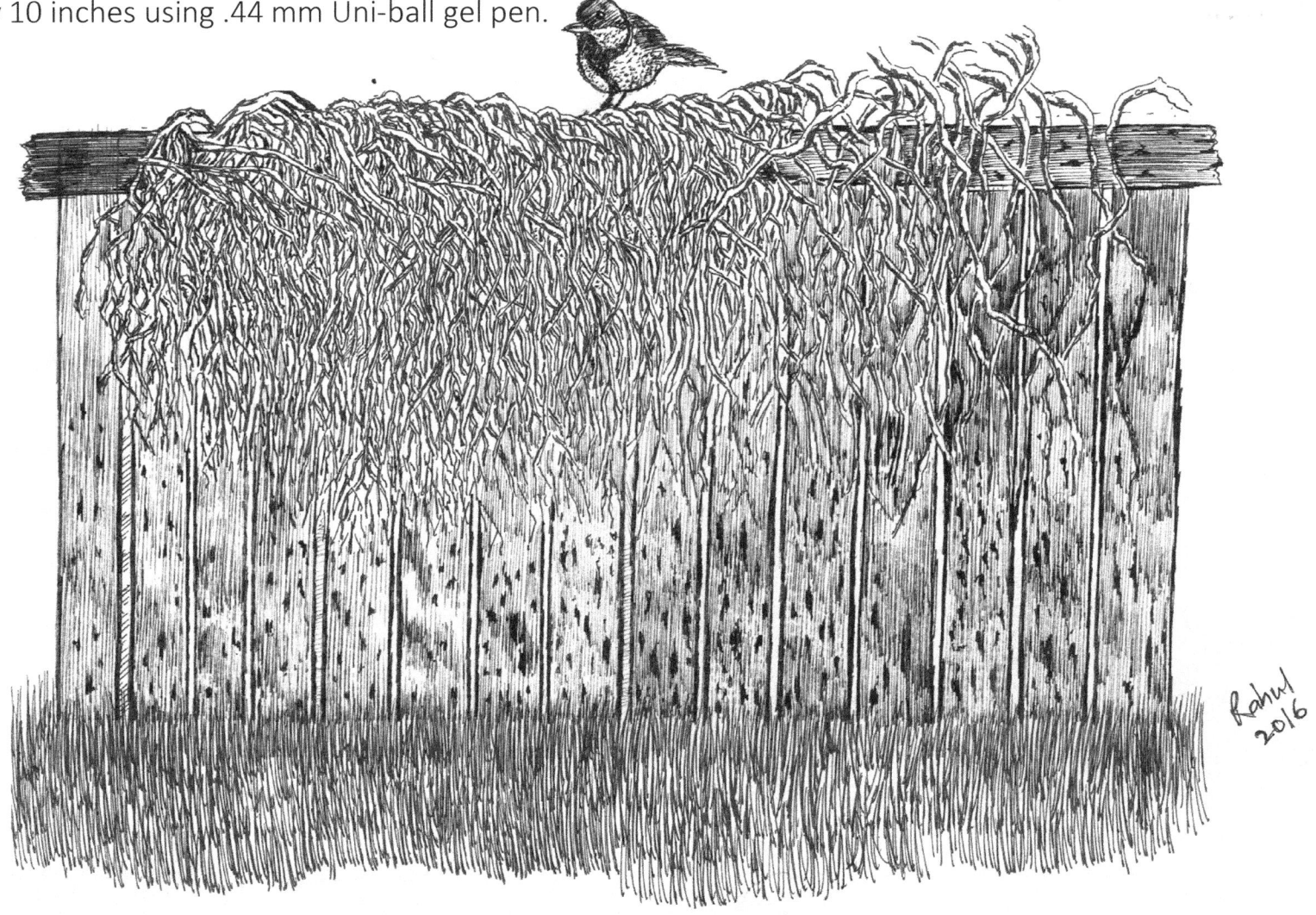

Drawing A Simple Wooden Scene:

The techniques we learnt in drawing vines over a fence can be used to draw a wooded scene as well and this is discussed next. The key idea is to always start by drawing few main foreground twigs/trunks and successively add overlapping other twigs/trunks and foliage in space between to create depth.

Make sure to use 'organic line' as discussed earlier to draw the outlines of twigs and trunks.

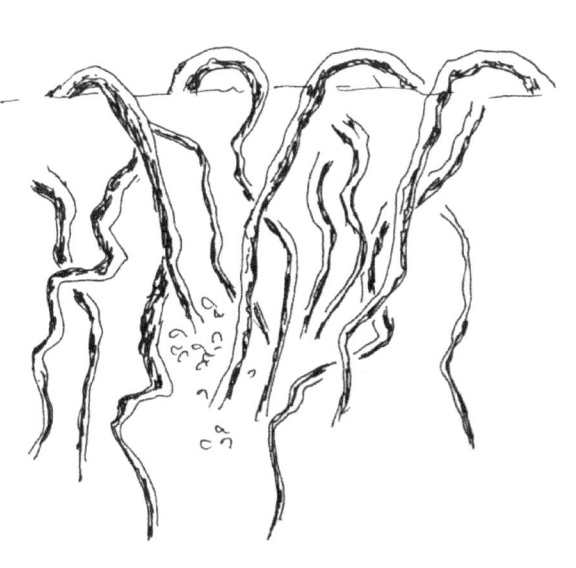

Vines/Twigs over a fence
(goes top to bottom)

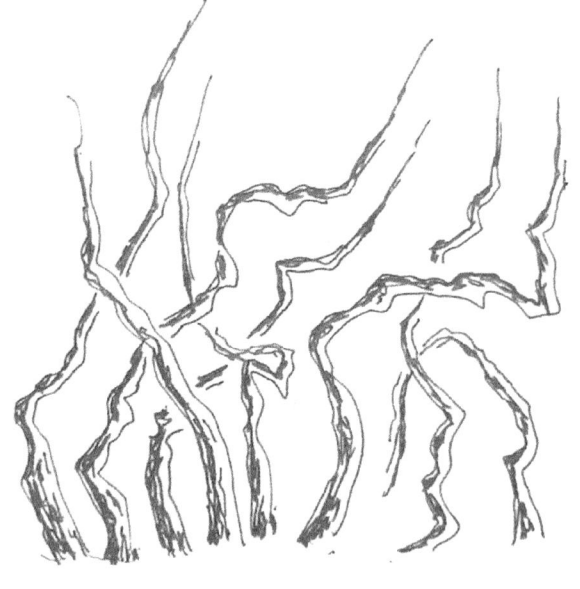

Vertical Twigs and Twisted
trunks (bottom to top)

Drawing A Simple Wooden Scene:

Here instead of drawing over a fence, same technique as in last example is used to draw twisted trunks from the ground for a wooded scene.

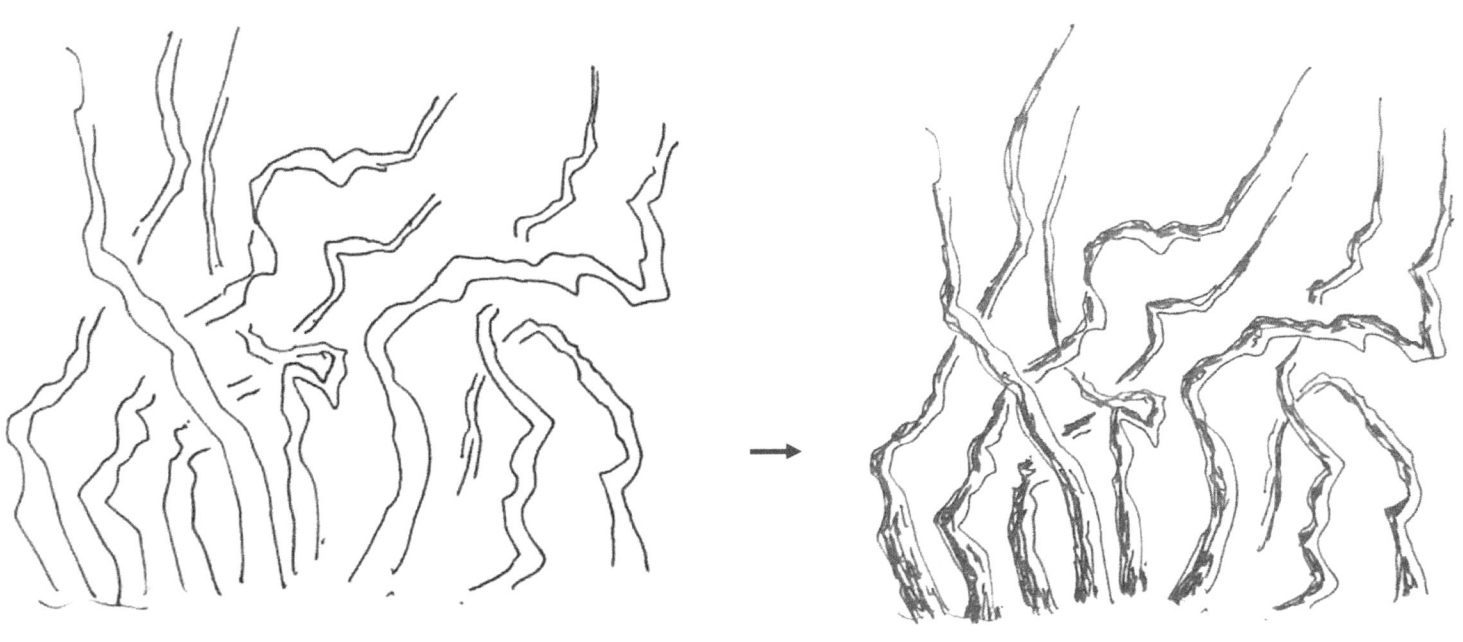

Start by drawing the foreground trunks.

Texture them using 2 tone technique as discussed earlier.

Drawing A Simple Wooden Scene, Completed:

By varying the density of trunks and their size and shape, different feel for wooded scenes can be obtained using this technique.

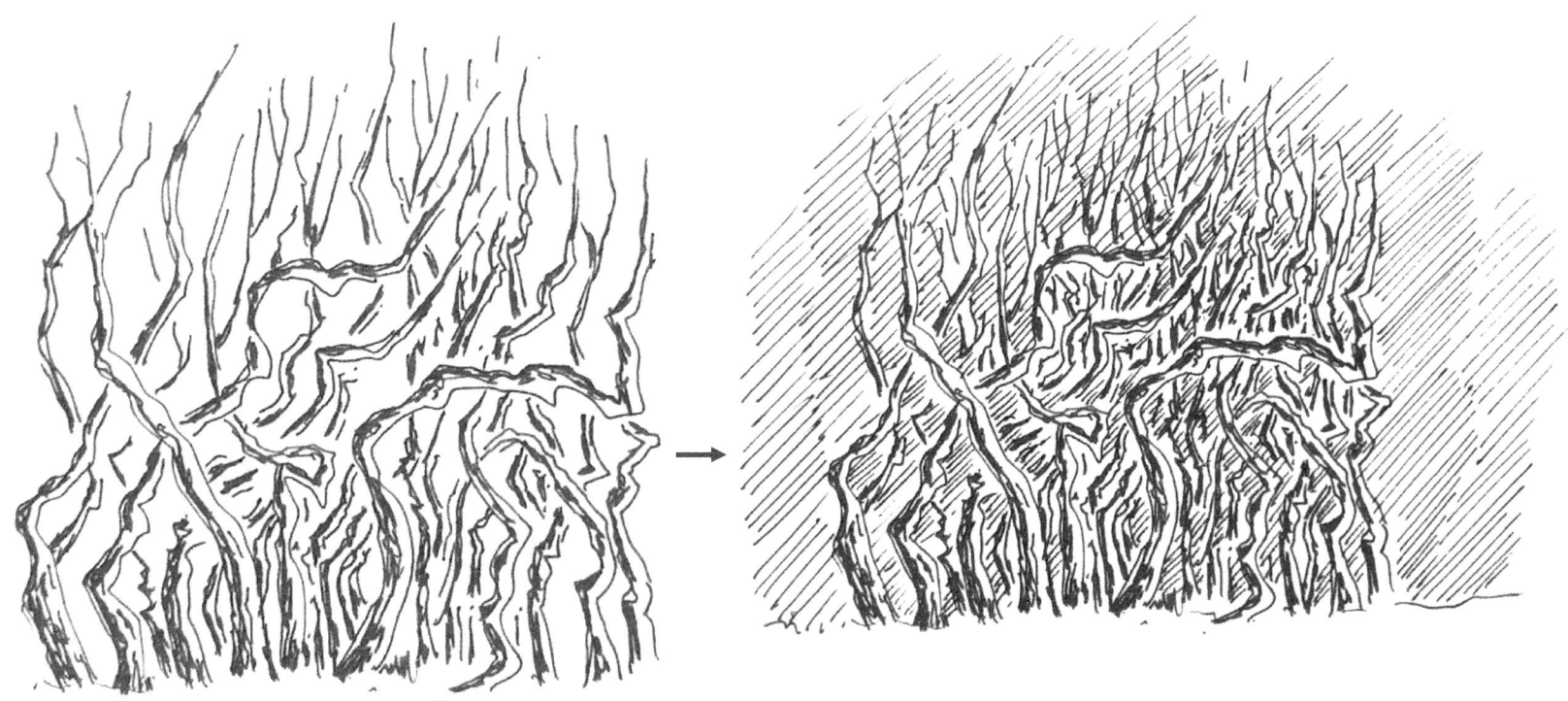

Add smaller trunks in between to give it a nice feel.

Angular parallel lines are a great way to create a pleasant backdrop for a wooded scene. Without foliage, it gives a feel of winter setting.

Adding A Backdrop for a Wooden Scene:

Unless the wooded scene extends to all of the drawing area, Without some kind of backdrop, a wooded scene looks unfinished against the white of the paper. A simple approach is to use angular parallel lines to provide a place for our eyes to rest as a backdrop. Use of other elements to provide a backdrop and add interest is discussed later.

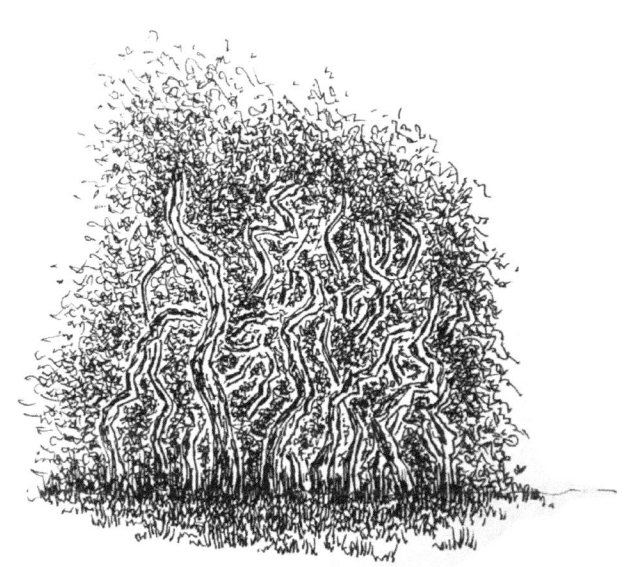

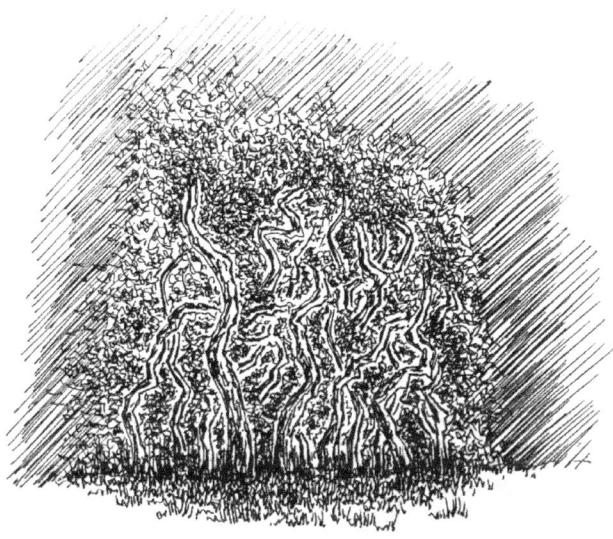

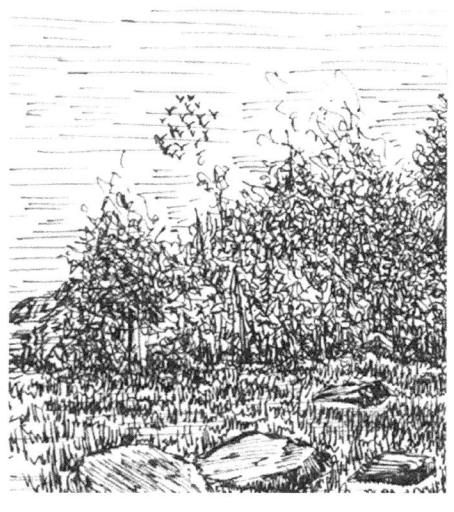

Without a background, the white of paper contrasts with a wooded scene and gives an unfinished feel.

Adding angular parallel lines gives a nice backdrop and a transition from wooded area to something in the back

Another option is to draw clouds/Sky and other distant elements to give a finished feel.

Drawing other elements like sky, mountains, hills etc. to give a nice backdrop and make a wooded area more pleasing is discussed in other volumes in the series at www.pendrawings.me/workbooks.

Drawing A Simple Wooden Scene with Dense Foliage:

Instead of adding more density of trunks, more foliage can instead be added to create a different feel for the wooded scene. This is similar to what we did for drawing vines before.

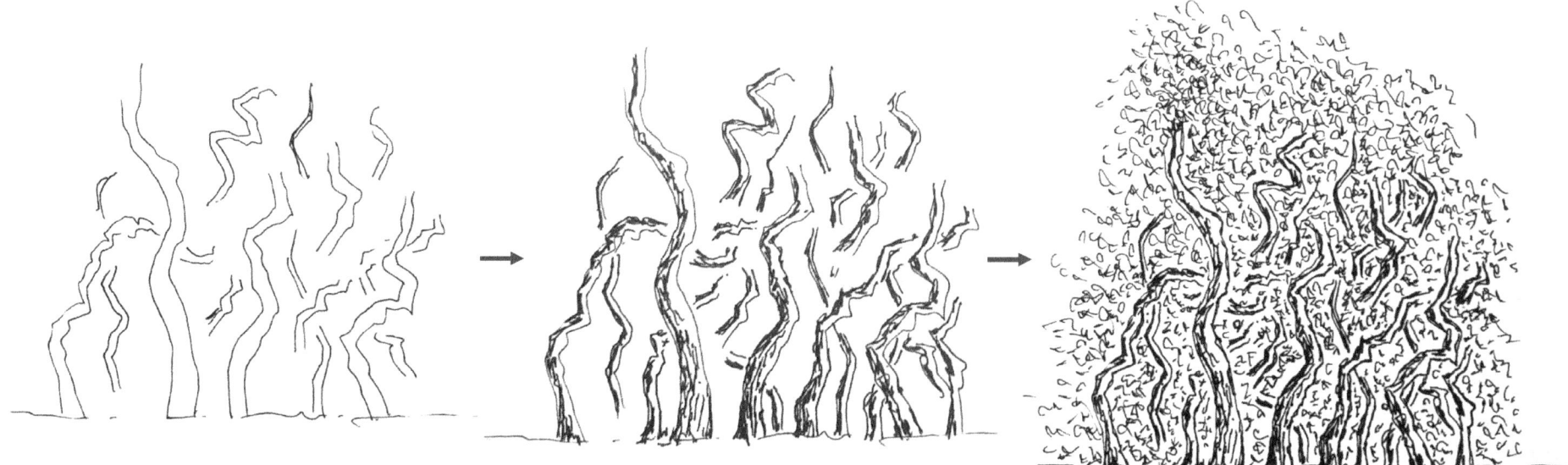

After some overlapping foreground trunks are drawn, space between is filled with foliage instead of more trunks.

Drawing A Simple Wooden Scene with Dense Foliage, Completed:

This results in a wooded scene with more feel of foliage.

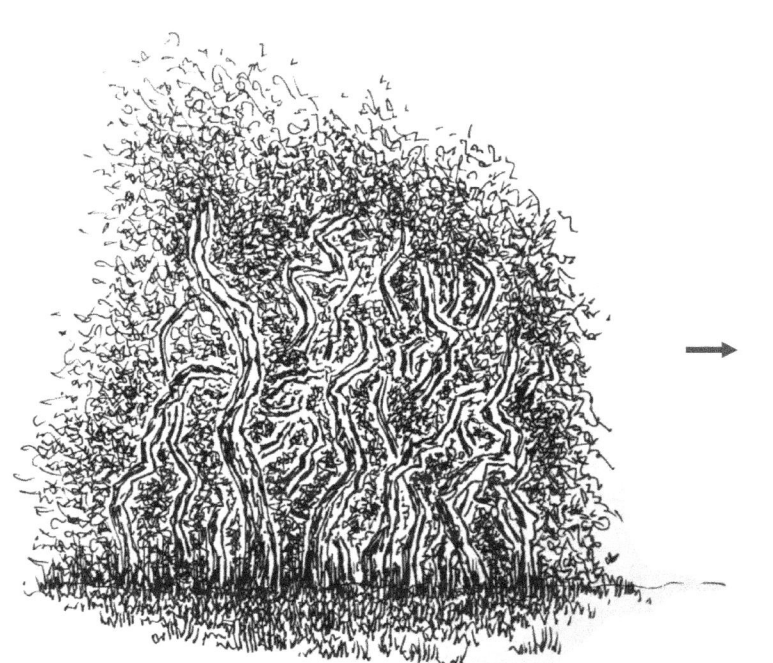

Use more foliage stroke to create higher density of foliage. Make sure there is a variation in density of foliage to bring out depth

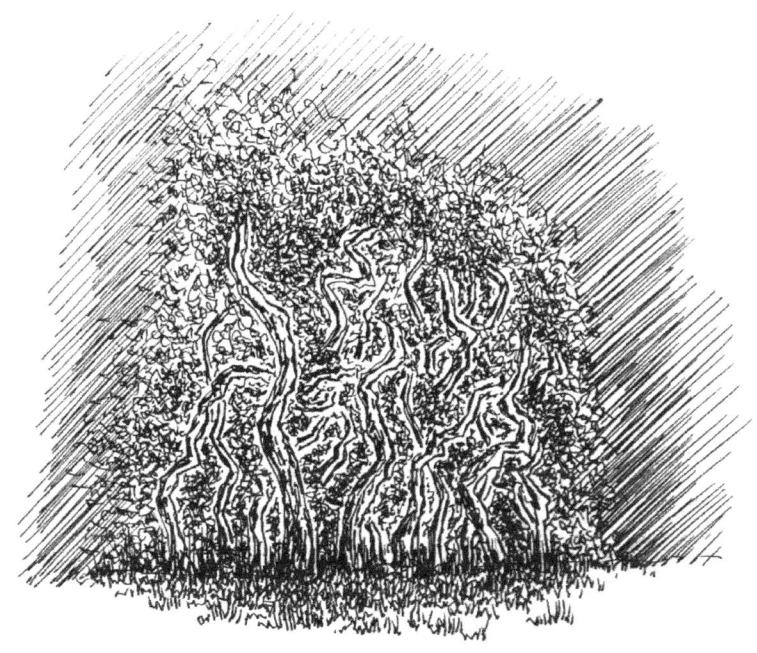

A backdrop of parallel lines gives a pleasant feel and makes the drawing look finished.

Drawing A Simple Wooden Scene with Scribble Foliage:

Here is another example to study where Scribble stroke is used to draw foliage.

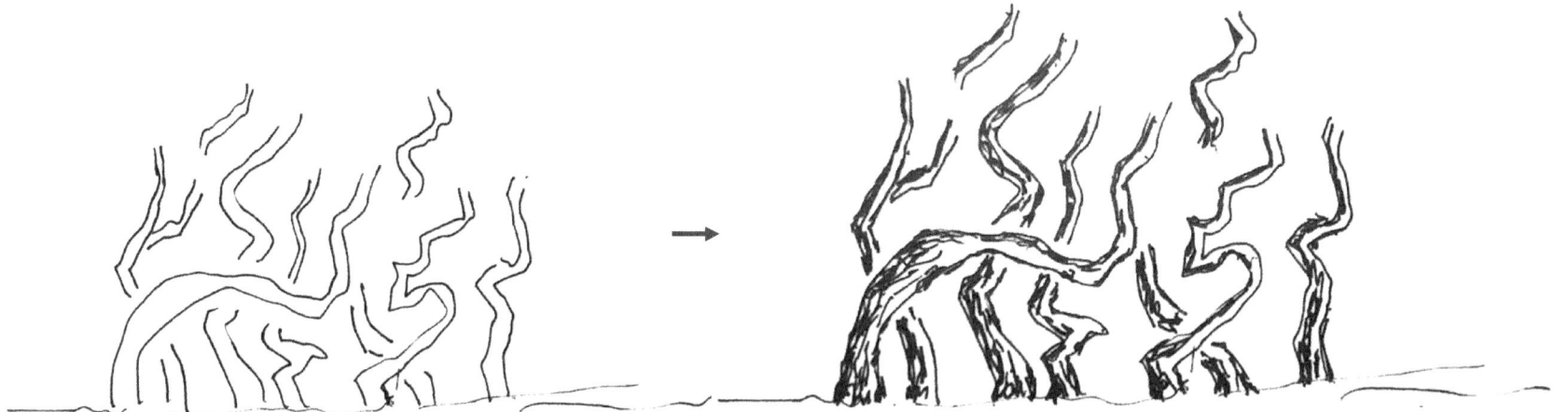

Start by using organic lines to draw outlines of overlapping twisted trunks/twigs and texture them using 2 tone technique.

Drawing A Simple Wooden Scene with Scribble Foliage, Completed:

Scribble stroke is used to draw foliage. More stroke is used to vary foliage density to add depth as discussed before.

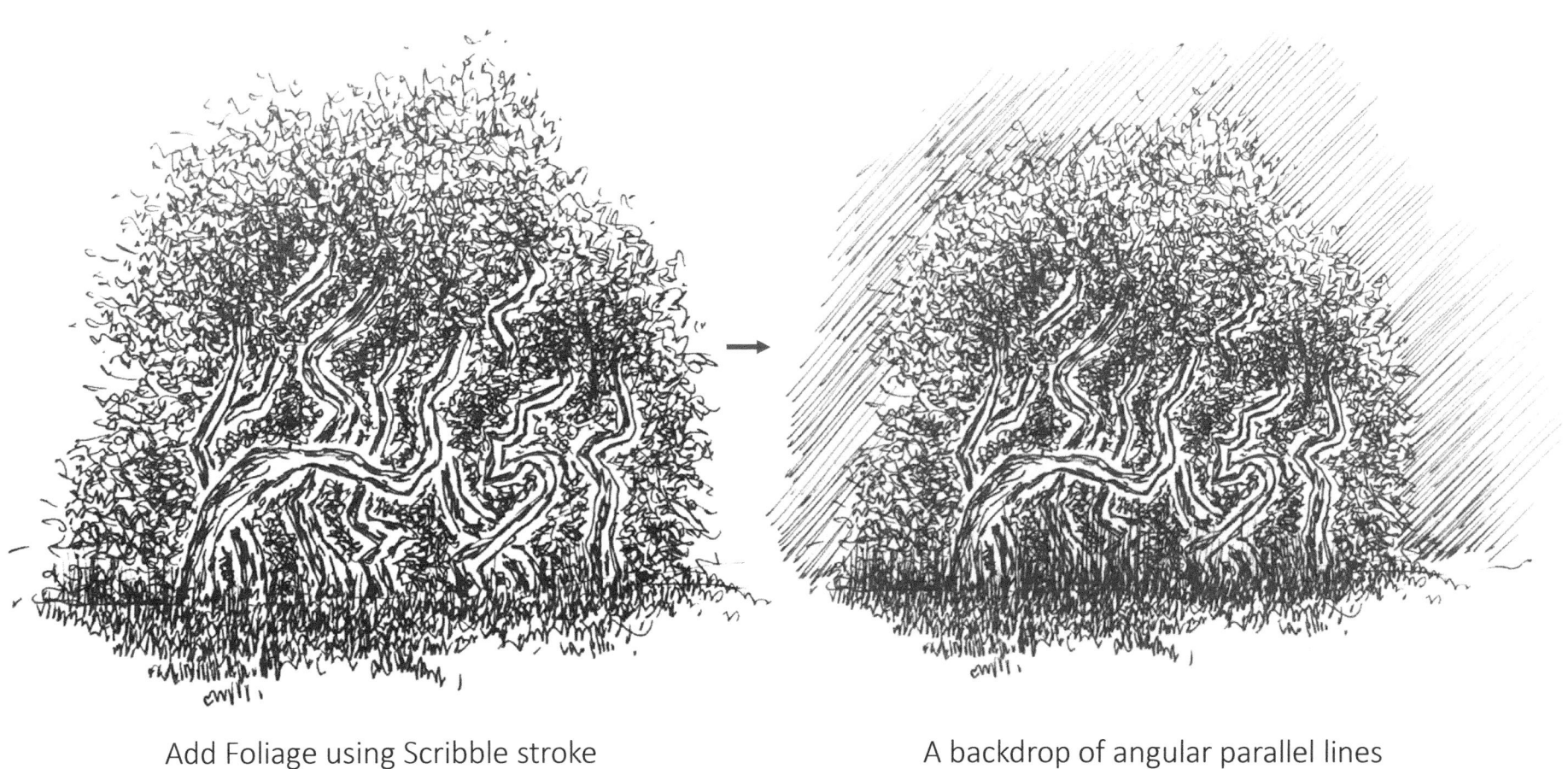

Add Foliage using Scribble stroke and vary the foliage density.

A backdrop of angular parallel lines again provides a finished feel.

Drawing A Simple Wooden Scene with Loopy Stroke for Foliage:

In this example, Loopy stoke as discussed earlier is used to draw foliage. Also, trunks are lot less intersecting and overlapping each other in this example and this gives it a different feel.

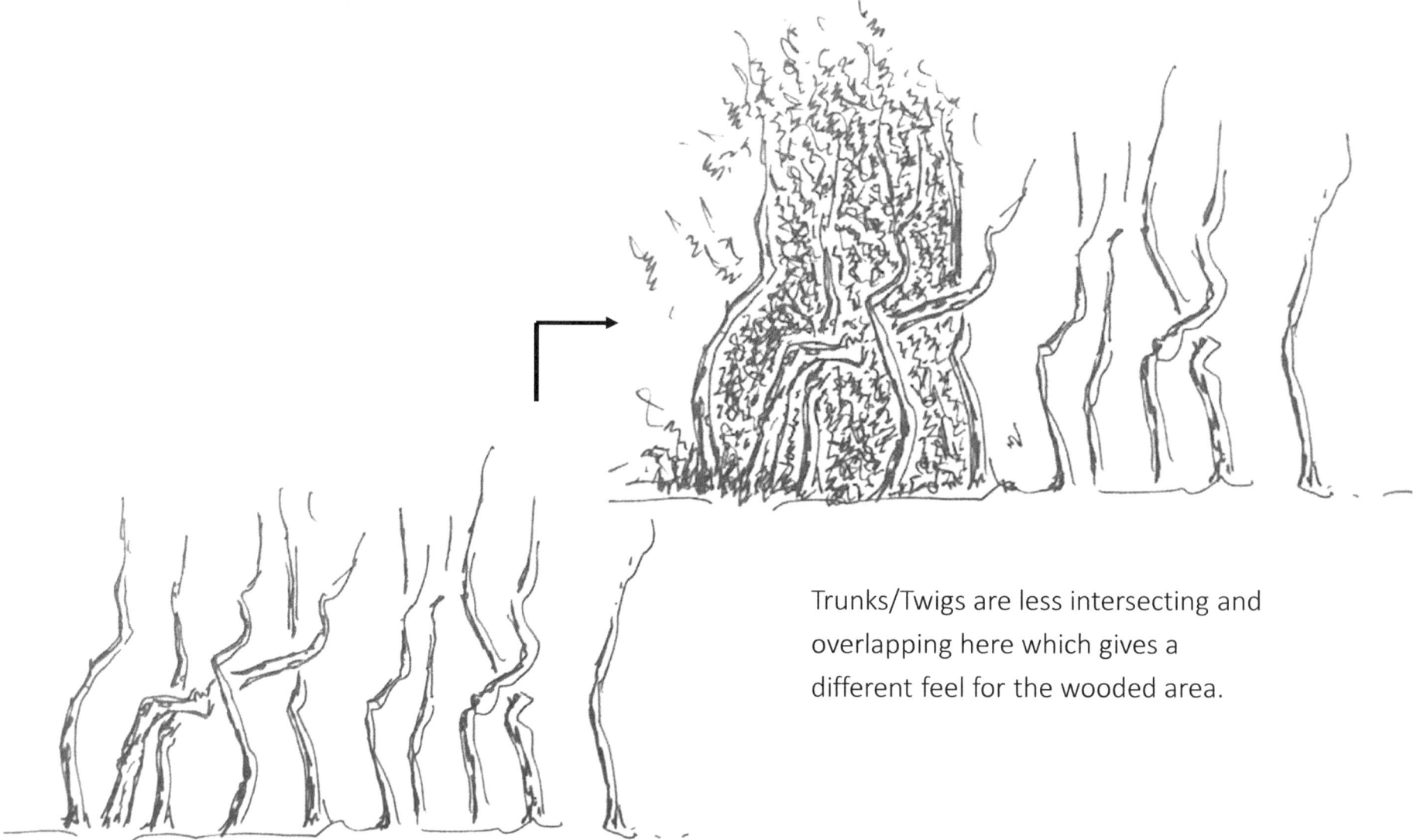

Trunks/Twigs are less intersecting and overlapping here which gives a different feel for the wooded area.

Drawing A Simple Wooden Scene with Loopy Stroke for Foliage, Completed:

Notice how use of Loopy stroke gives it a different feel. Also notice how absence of big dominant trunks gives it a different feel than the last drawing. Here thin trunks are used that don't stand out prominently compared to last drawing. Experiment with different sizes and distribution of trunks to get different feel for your drawings.

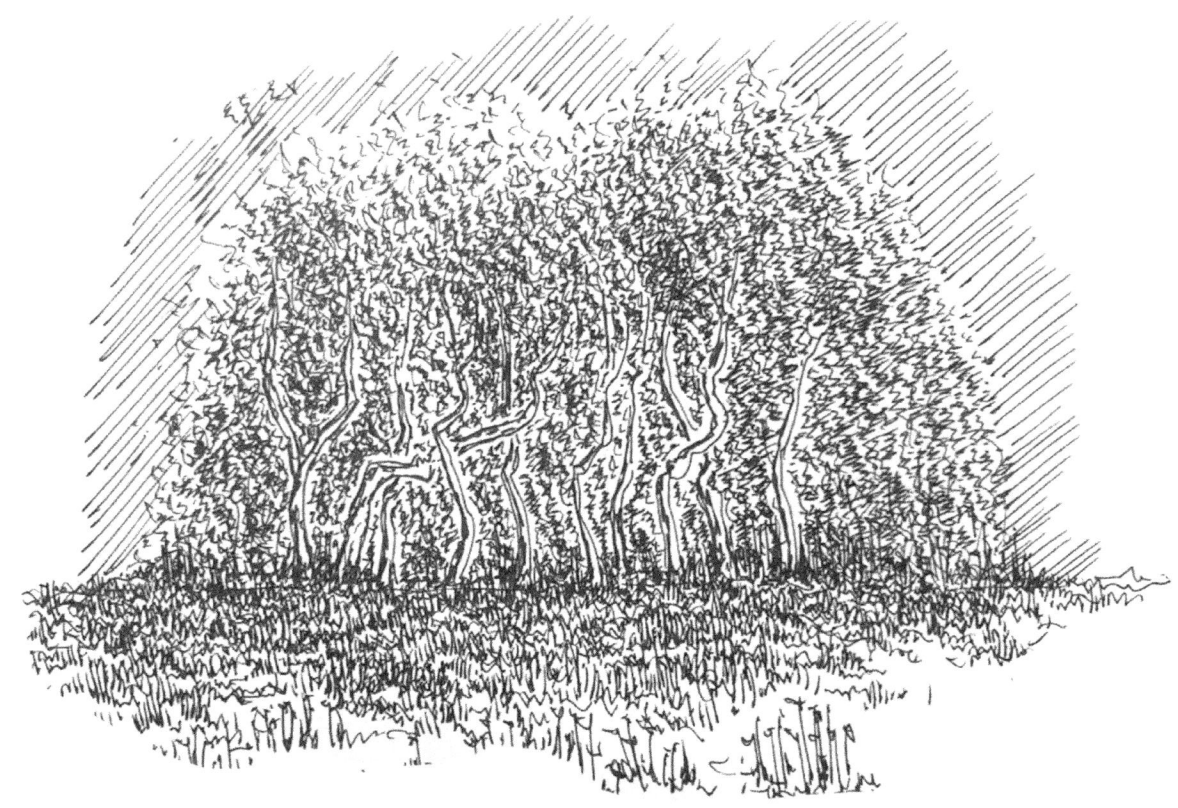

Relative Intensity of Darker Tone:

The level of darker tone in your drawing can make a big impact on the overall feel. Here is the same drawing as in last page but with higher level of foliage density giving it a more darker tone. Also the texturing of twigs/trunks is done on the darker end giving a more intense feel to this drawing compared to one on the previous page.

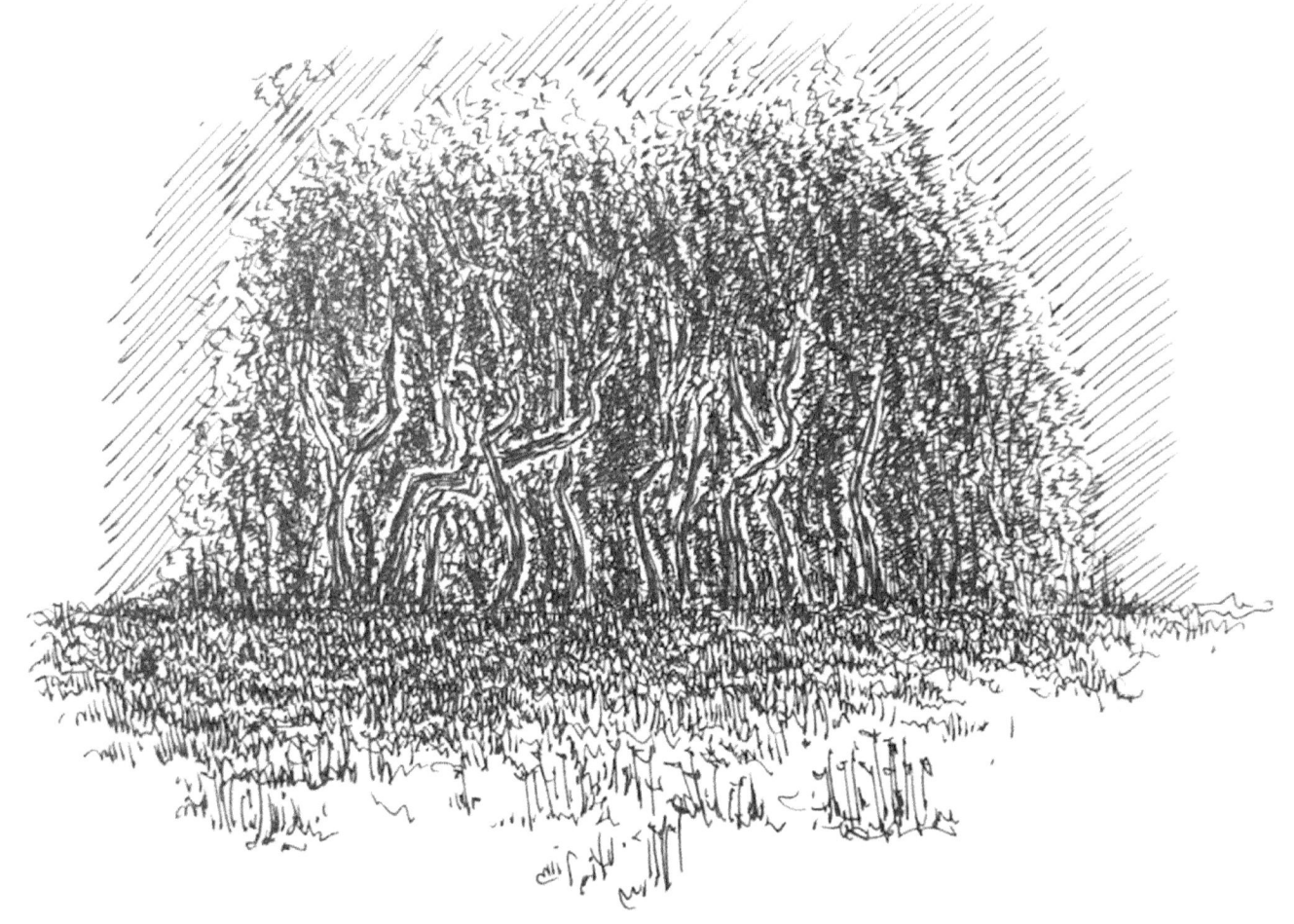

Importance of Leaving White:

In the absence of color in pen and ink drawing, it is very important to leave a small sliver of white between different elements, but especially between twigs/trunks and foliage for them to stand out. This becomes even more important as the digital image of a drawing is compressed to small size for online distribution and other purposes. Compression accentuates the darker tones and in the absence of small white between elements, the feel of drawing is often compromised.

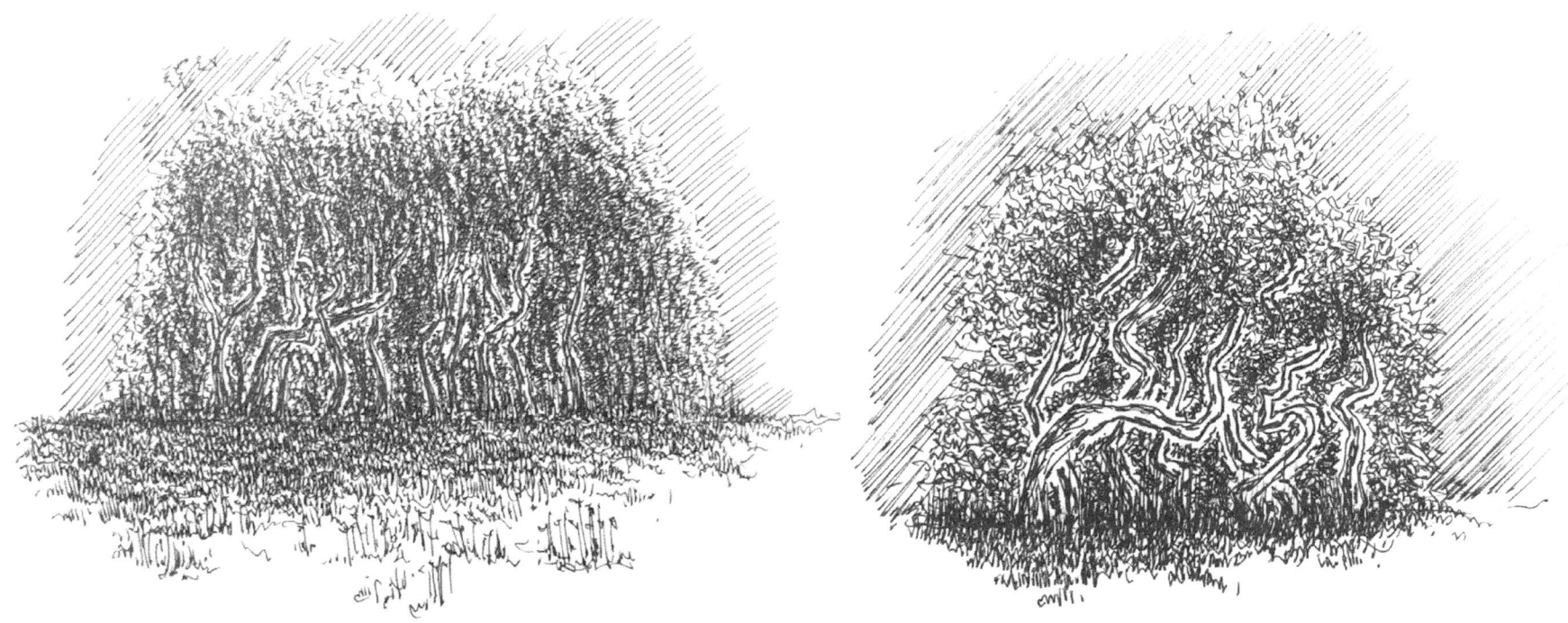

This is scaled down version of drawing on the last page. Notice how the small white between trunks and foliage still stands out and keeps the wooded feel intact.

The white between the foreground trunks and foliage is accentuated on compression and gives more dramatic feel to the drawing.

Some Examples:

Here are some examples with more details. The technique is the same as discussed before. They are drawn bigger than printed here. Once you get comfortable with the technique, such drawings can be attempted.

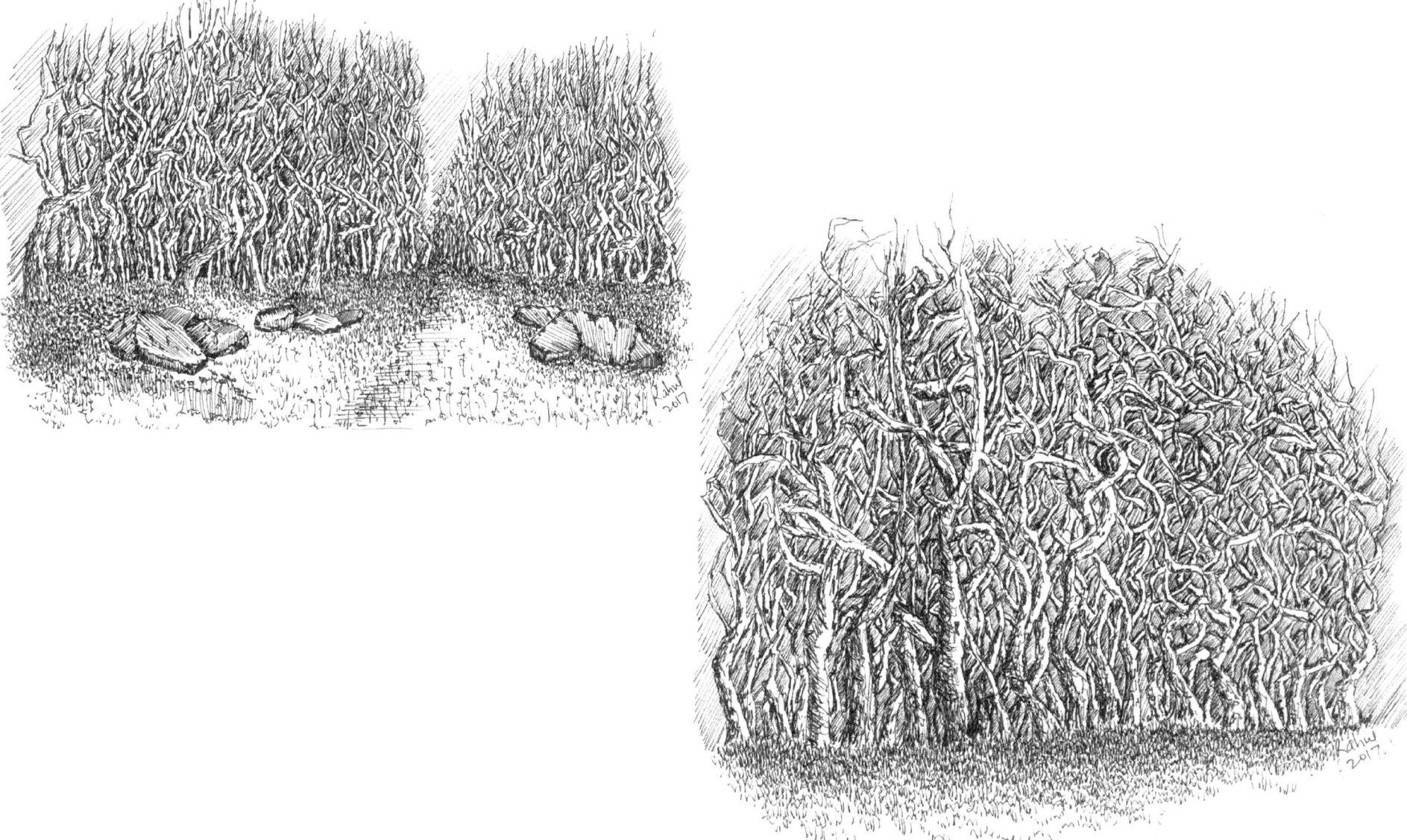

Alternate Approach to Drawing A Foliage Heavy Wooded Scene:

In the previous techniques, foreground trunks and twigs etc. were textured initially and foliage drawn around them. This enabled us to choose the level of texturing and tone we wanted to use for them and highlight them appropriately. An alternate approach is to cover the area with foliage initially and draw the trunks and twigs as solid tapered darks. This gives a different feel but very pleasing effect when done properly.

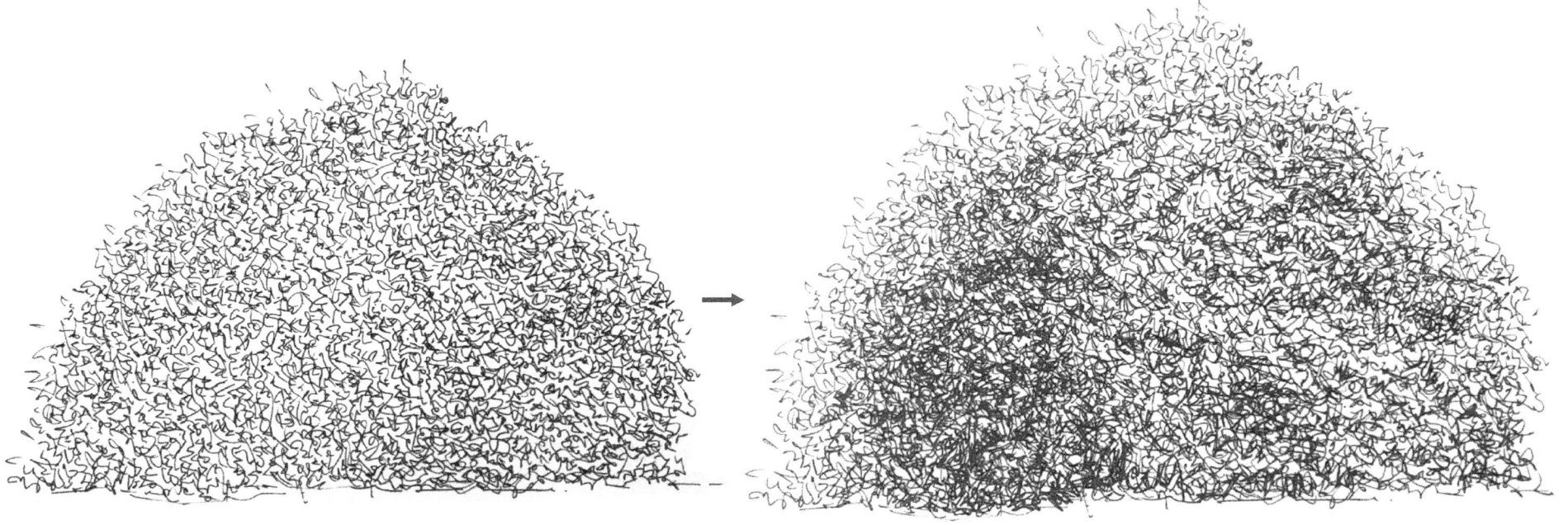

Start by drawing a layer of foliage. Here scribble stroke is used.

Use more scribble stroke to add tonal variation. Make sure it feels random to bring out the depth and the feel of foliage as shown above.

Importance of Randomness in Foliage Tonal Distribution:

When adding tonal variation to foliage, it is very important to make sure that it feels random and there are no specific lines or patterns that are visible. Presence of any specific lines in tonal change will destroy the foliage effect. The best way to achieve this is to jump from one area to another and keep your hands moving. Add a little bit of tone here, a little there and moving your hands around in this manner will avoid any repetition or emergence of a pattern.

Initial Layer of Foliage.

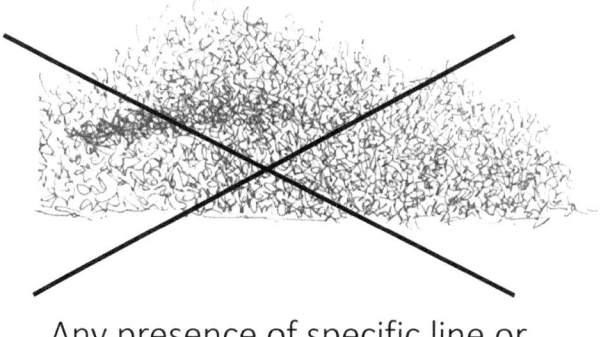

Any presence of specific line or pattern in adding tone will destroy the foliage effect.

Keep your hand moving and add tonal distribution in this random manner to bring out the depth. It takes some practice. The key is to add tones to different areas in random manner.

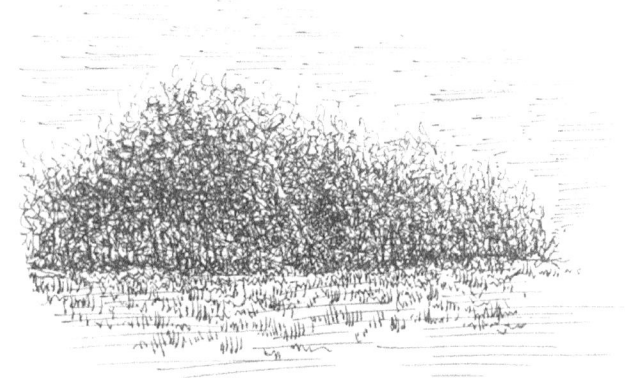

Alternate Approach to Drawing A Foliage Heavy Wooded Scene, Continued:

Just by using scribble stroke and creating interesting tonal variations in the foliage, a pleasing wooded setting can be drawn as seen below.

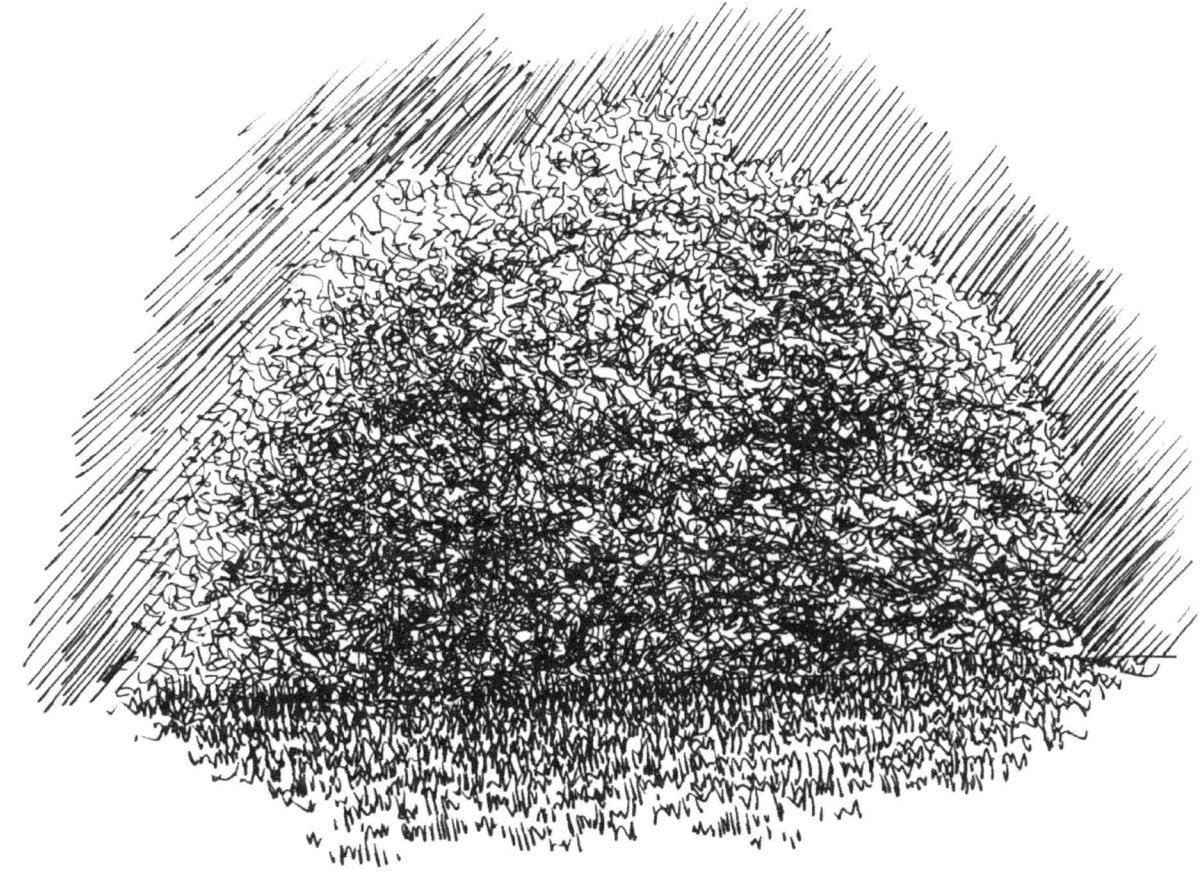

Add a backdrop of angled parallel lines and ground cover to give it a finished feel.

Alternate Approach to Drawing A Foliage Heavy Wooded Scene, Finished:

Trunks and twigs etc. are added as solid tapered darks in this technique. As there is no 'erasing' of foliage that is drawn initially, the trunks and twigs can only be textured over the foliage as solid darks. This recedes them a bit (moves to the background) compared to technique where they are drawn initially but still gives very pleasing feel.

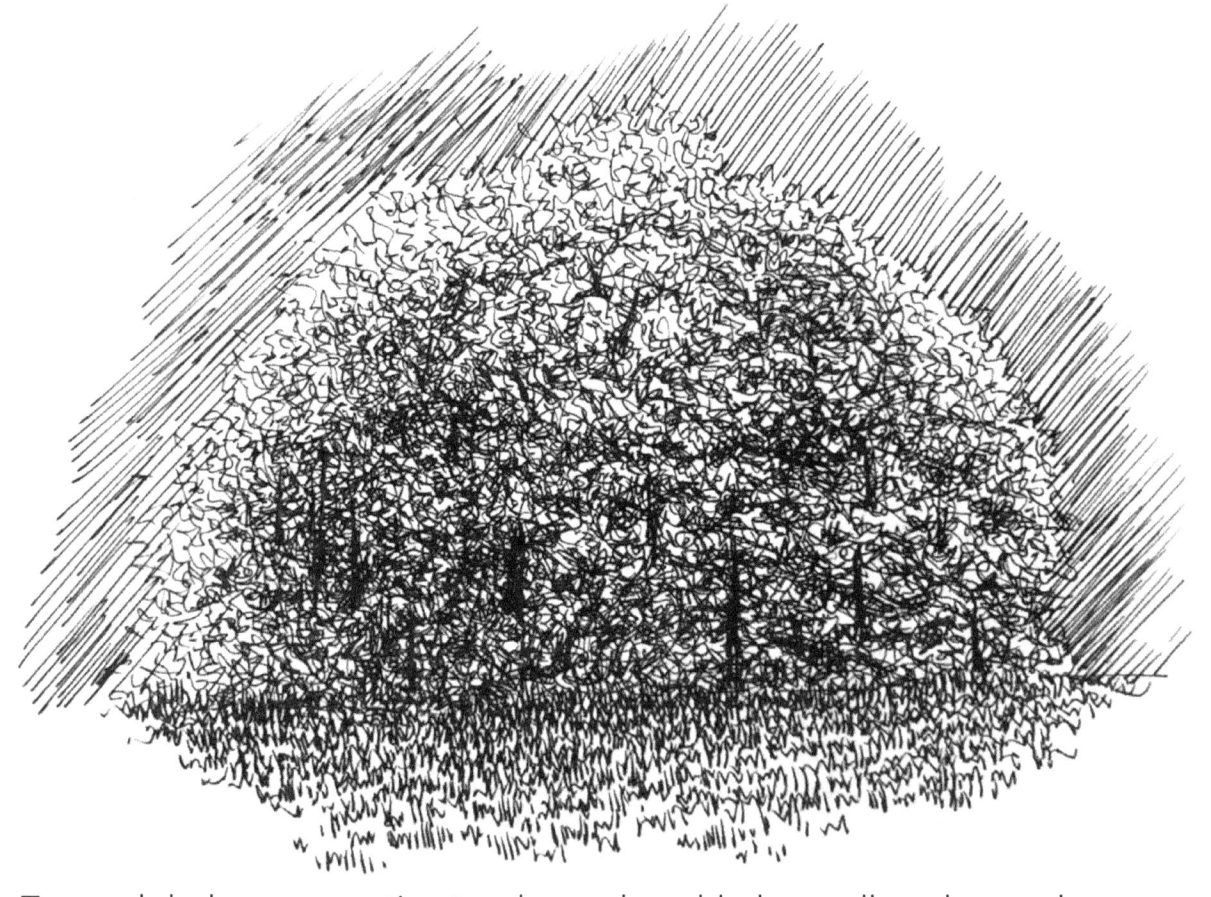

Tapered darks representing trunks can be added as well as shown above
to further give it a wooded feel.

Another Example of Foliage Heavy Wooded Scene with Scribble Stroke:

The technique discussed last is very powerful and by using different shape and density of scribble foliage, attractive wooden scenes can be quickly done. Here is another example.

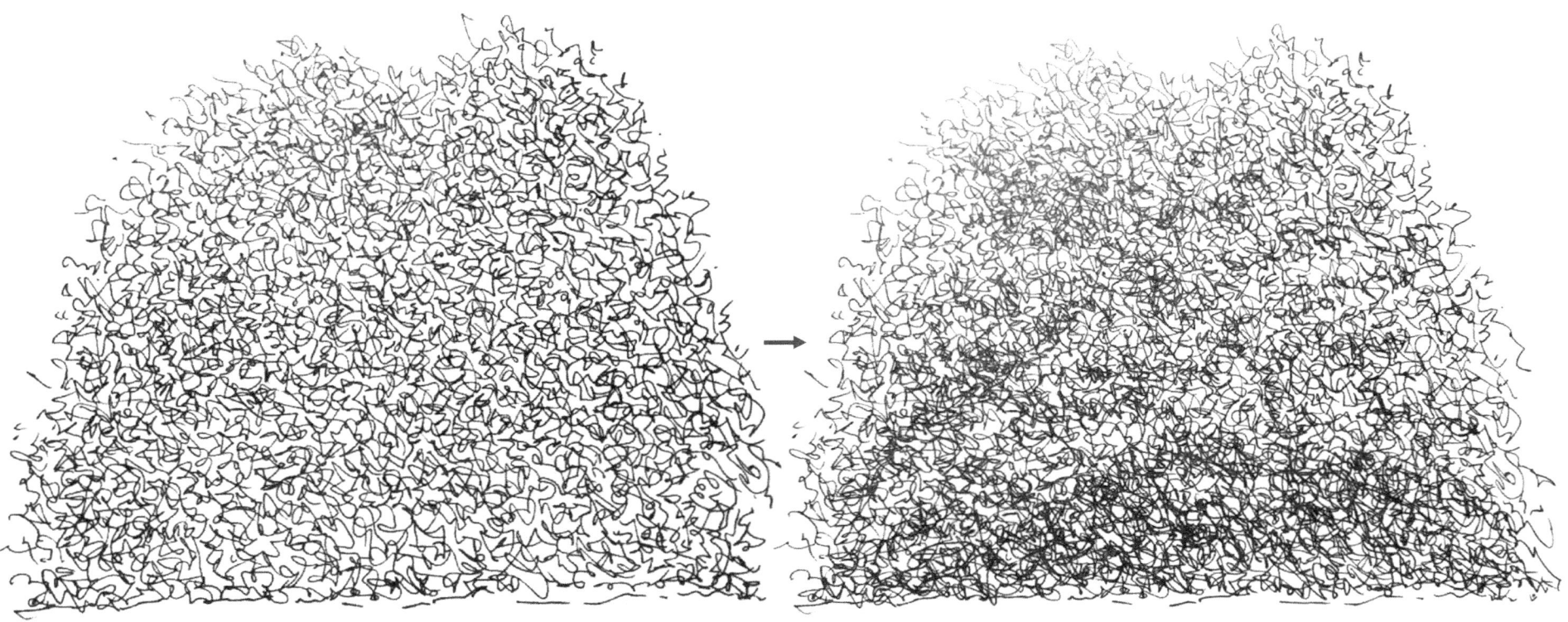

As before, start by drawing a layer of scribble foliage. Next add tonal variations randomly by using additional scribble strokes as shown above

A Foliage Heavy Wooded Scene with Scribble Stroke, Continued:

Deep darks in few places in foliage really helps to bring out depth and adds interest to the drawing.

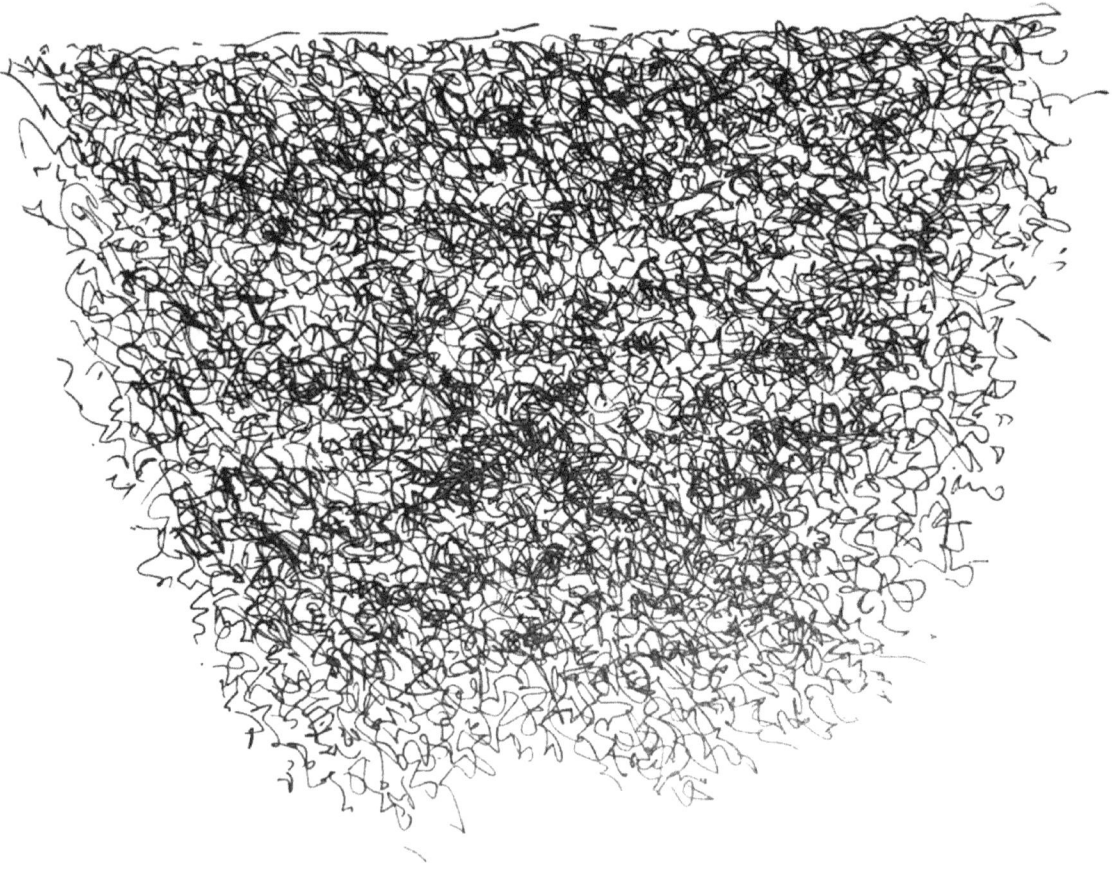

Use additional scribble foliage stroke to make some parts dark in irregular manner. Such tonal variation is very important to bring out the depth in the drawing.

A Foliage Heavy Wooded Scene with Scribble Stroke, Completed:

Add indication of trunks as solid tapered darks. In this example, more trunks are used compared to last example and this gives a different feel. Experiment with combination of different levels of foliage and trunks in your attempts to see what you like.

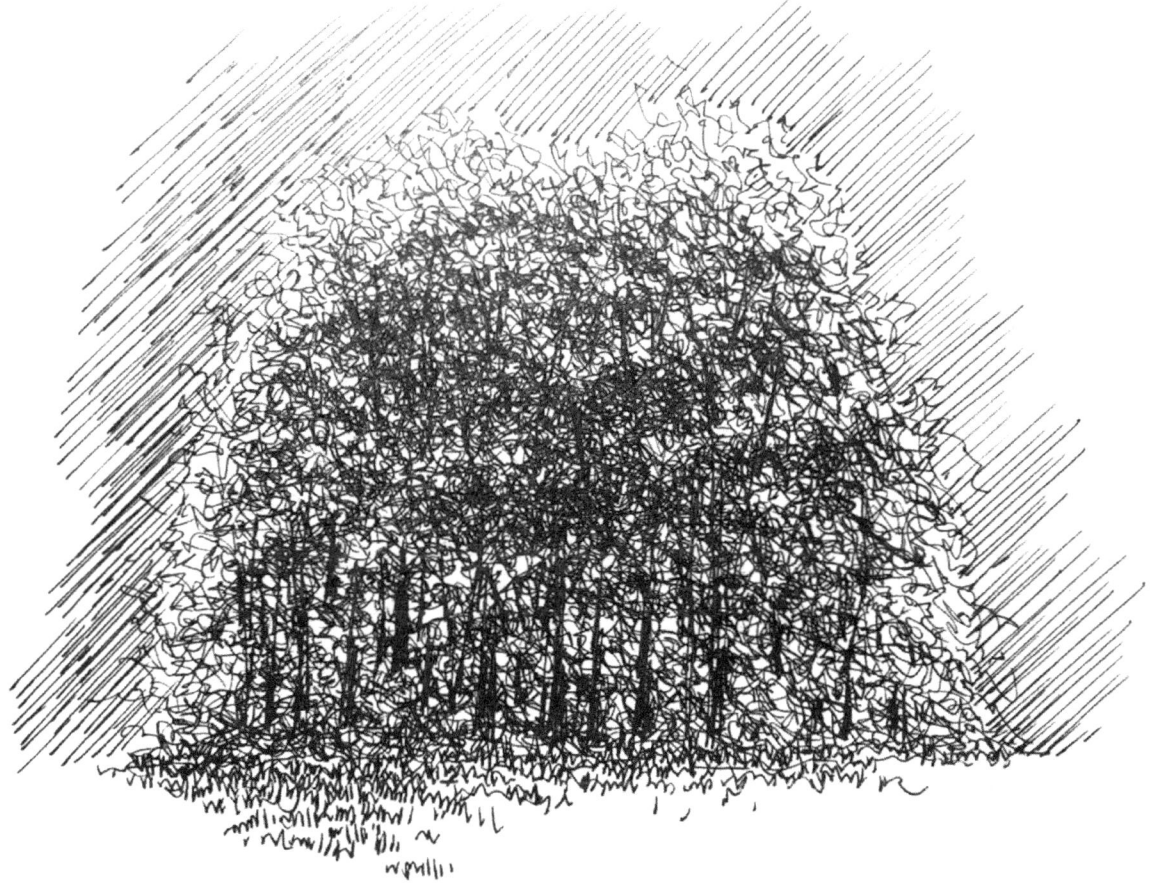

Use of intense dark areas, as done above, helps to make the drawing more dramatic and draws viewer's interest. Make sure not to over use it but do so in a controlled manner to provide contrast. Trunks are also added as solid tapered darks to further add depth and interest to the drawing.

Yet Another Example with Loopy Stroke:

Here is another example where loopy foliage stroke as discussed earlier is used to draw foliage and create wooded setting using technique discussed last. By using different foliage strokes, shapes and density of foliage and trunks, very different drawings can be done using this technique.

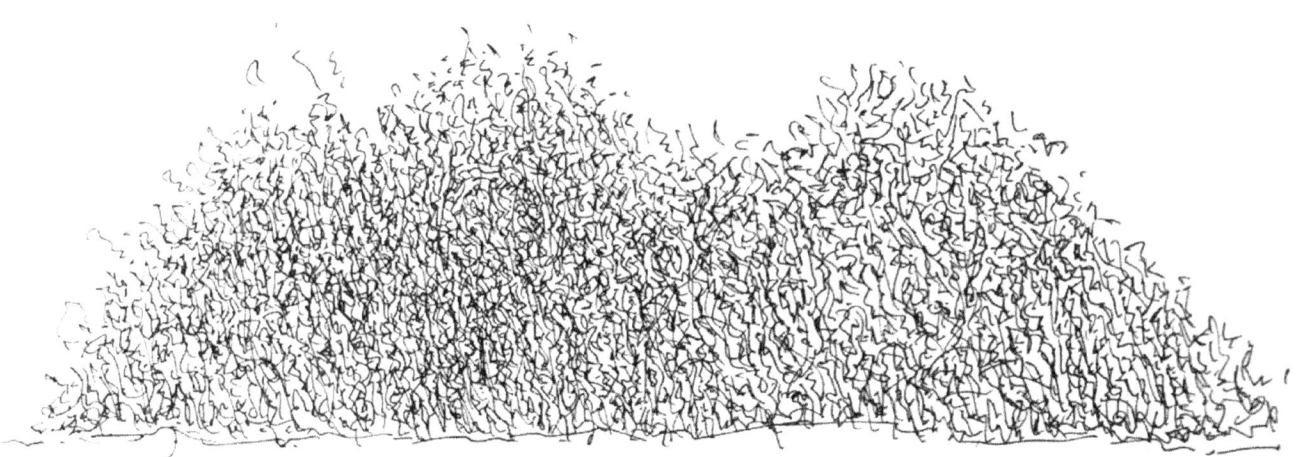

As before, start by drawing a layer of foliage. Here Loopy Stroke is used to draw initial layer of Foliage

Yet Another Example with Loopy Stroke Continued:

Use more stroke to add tonal variation to the foliage. As discussed before, this is very important to add depth to the drawing. Darker areas are perceived as in the back (background) and lighter areas more to the front. Such tonal variation causes different areas to be perceived as back or front based on their tones and adds depth to the drawing.

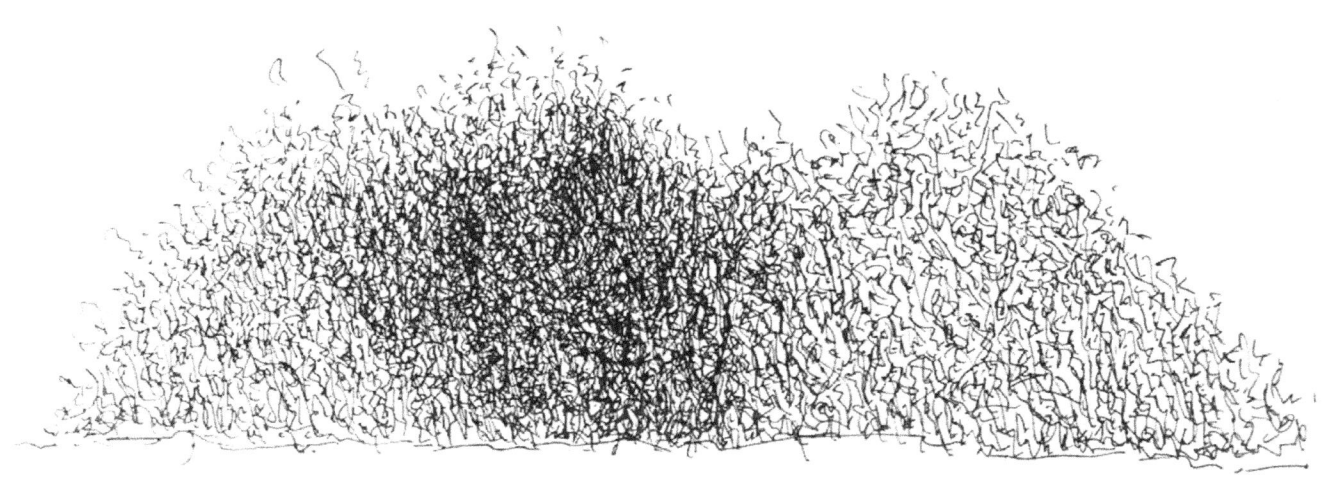

Use more stroke to add tonal variation in an irregular manner.

Yet Another Example with Loopy Stroke Finished:

As before solid tapered trunks/twigs/branches can be added to make the drawing further interesting.

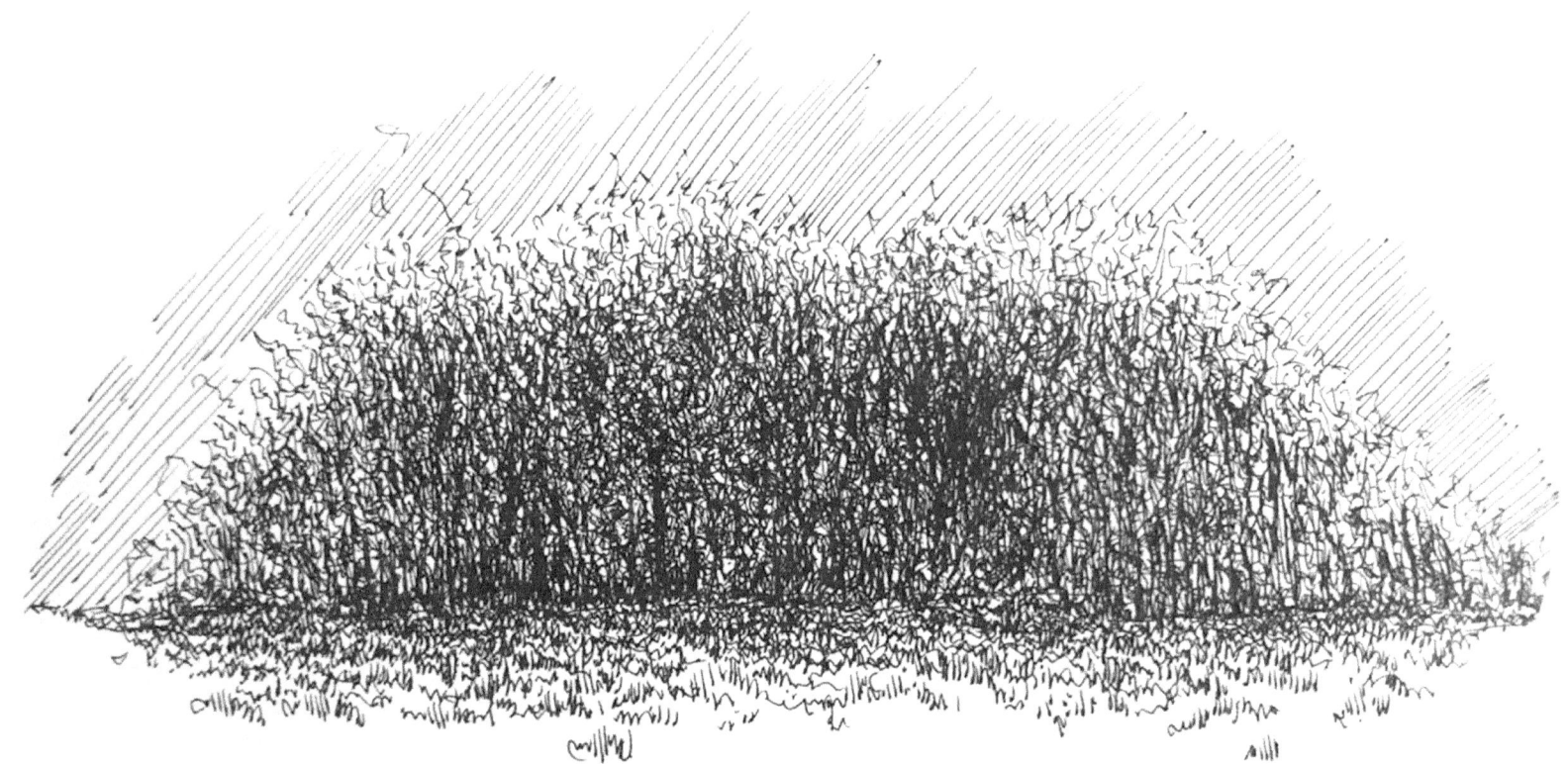

Here higher density of small trunks/twigs is used to create a different final feel.

Another Example:

As you practice drawing foliage and adding tonal variations, you will be able to bring out subtle tonal variations and create drawings with intensity.

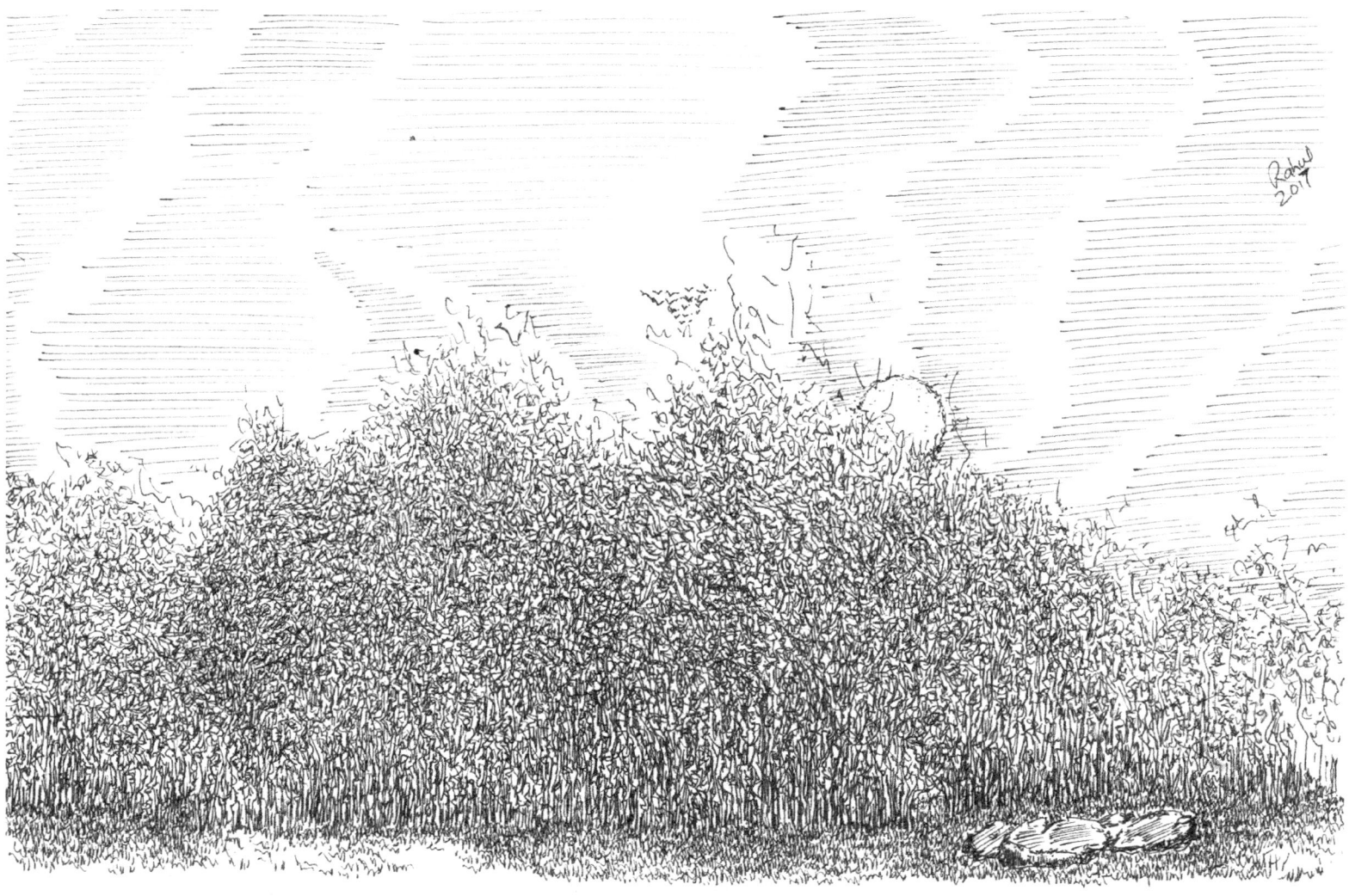

Activity: Drawing Wooded Area with Foliage:

Add more foliage stroke to bring out tonal variation and finish the following drawing as seen before.

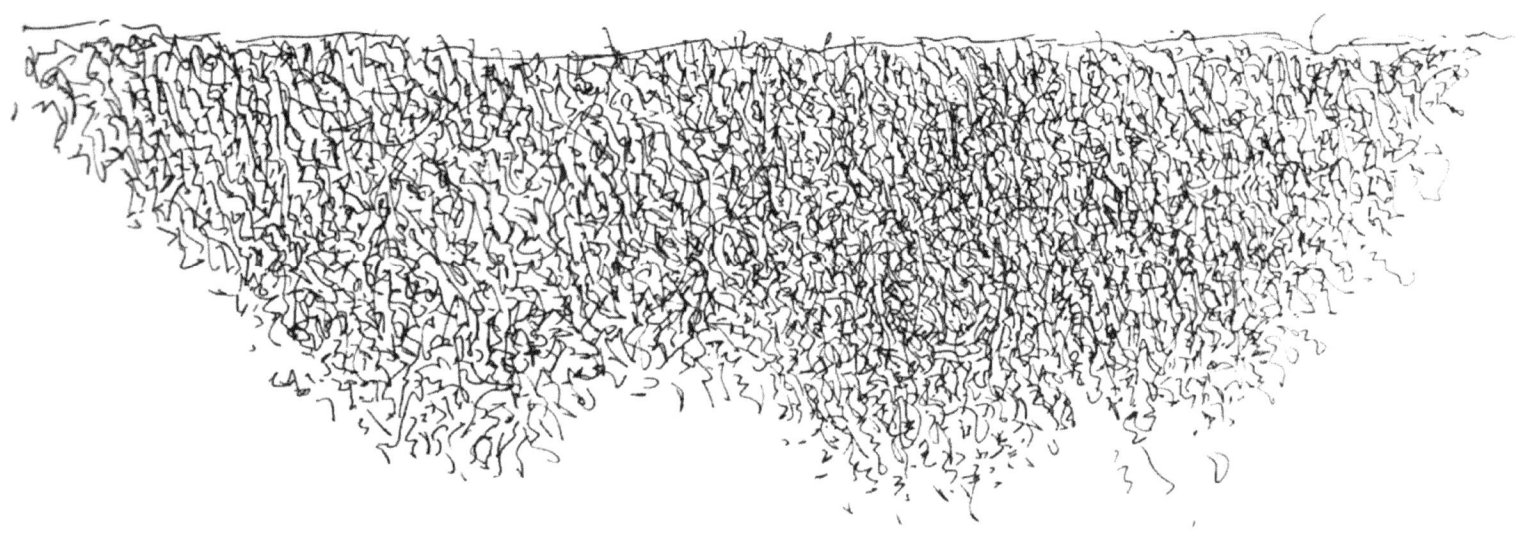

Having Fun with Pen Strokes:

As you get more comfortable with using pen, you can start to use different combination of strokes to create foliage. Any curvy open line as shown below conveys the effect of foliage. Notice below that I haven't used any one particular stroke in a repetitive manner but instead I have let my pen (and mind) wander and create strokes on the fly to convey foliage. This is the real joy of such drawings in that you can let your creative instincts flow and evolve your drawing with it.

Different types of pen strokes are used on the fly to create foliage.

Add such strokes in irregular manner to create tonal difference and depth.

Activity: Drawing Different Foliage Strokes:

Practice drawing different foliage strokes as shown below. Use different shapes and orientation to give it a nice organic feel.

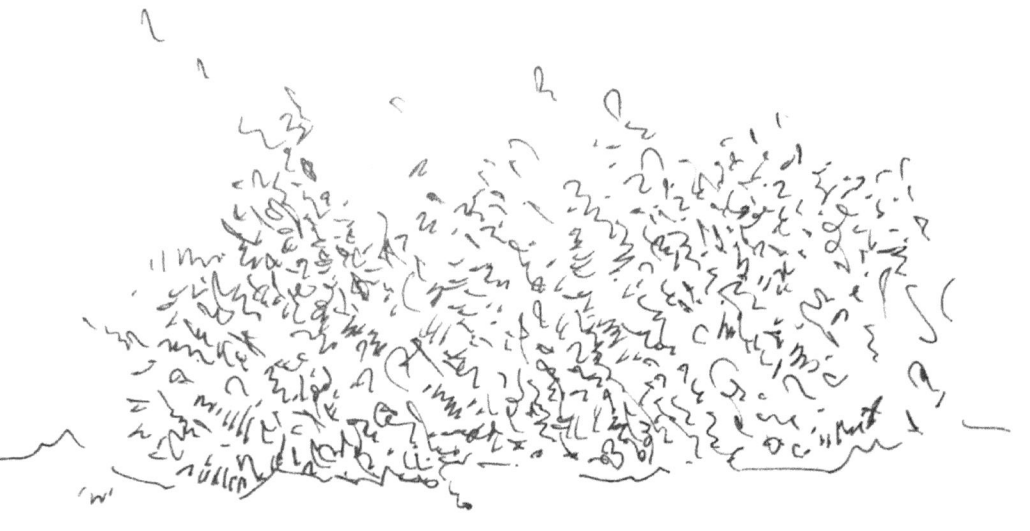

Having Fun with Pen Strokes, Completed:

Using such different combination of strokes creates very pleasing feel for foliage as can be seen below.

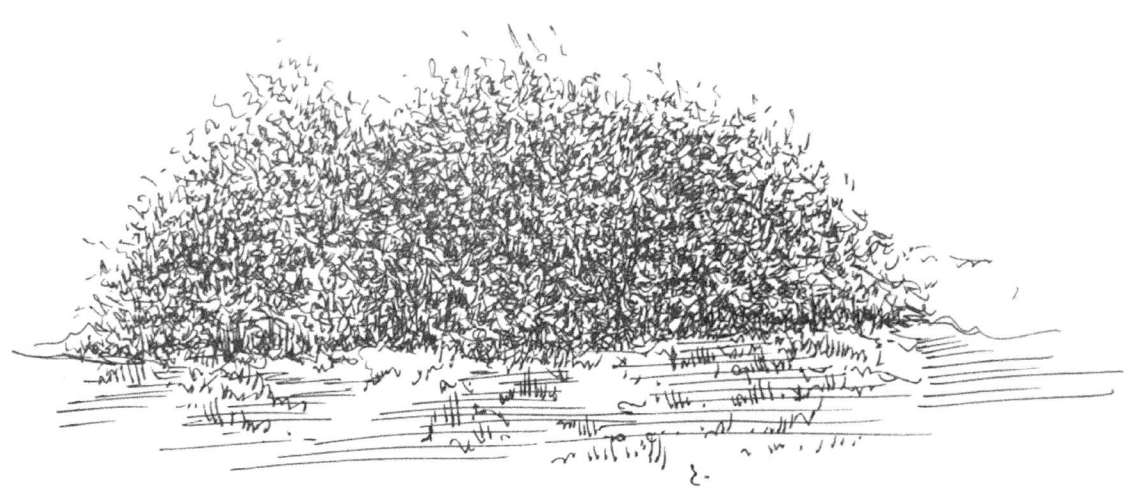

Use such different combination of strokes to create subtle tonal differences as shown above. This gives a very pleasing feel to the foliage.

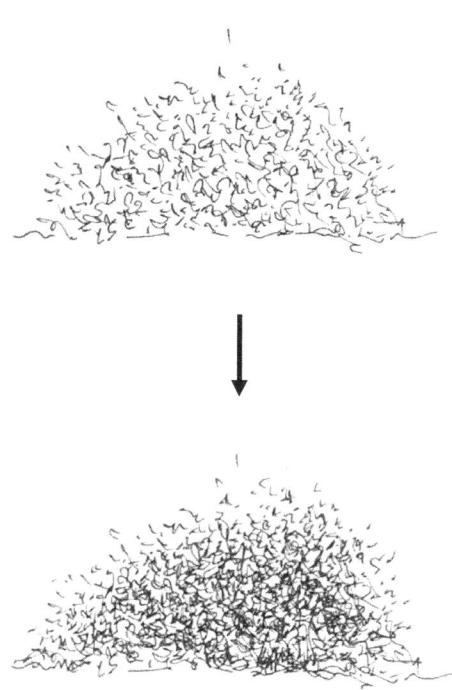

Here is another example.

Adding Other Elements:

To add more interest, other elements can be added to the wooded setting in the drawing. A simple approach is to provide a backdrop of distant tree line and mountains/hills in the distance. Adding Clouds/Sky and other foreground elements like stones, water, wooden posts etc. also add to the charm of the drawing. Below, other elements are added to the previous drawing to give it more visual interest.

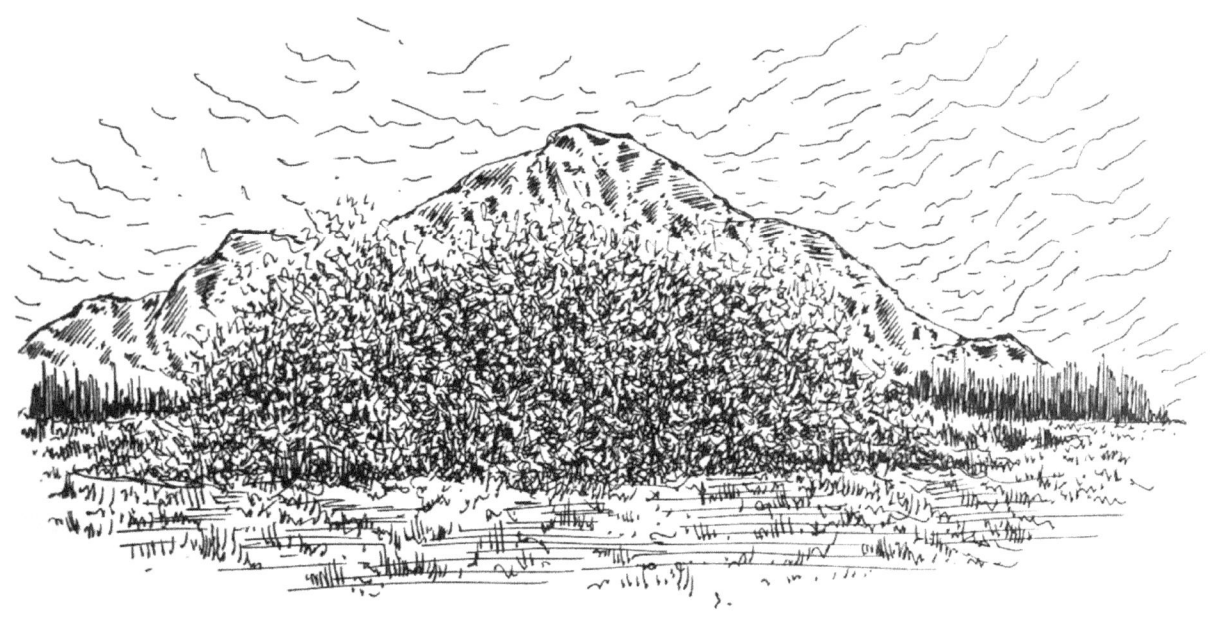

Drawing other elements of nature like mountains, sky, stones etc. is covered in other volumes in the series. Please visit **www.pendrawings.me/workbooks** for more information.

Adding Other Elements, Step by Step:

Following steps show a simple approach to adding other elements and incorporating a wooded area in your drawing. By using different combination on this theme, pleasing such drawings can be easily done from your imagination in short breaks.

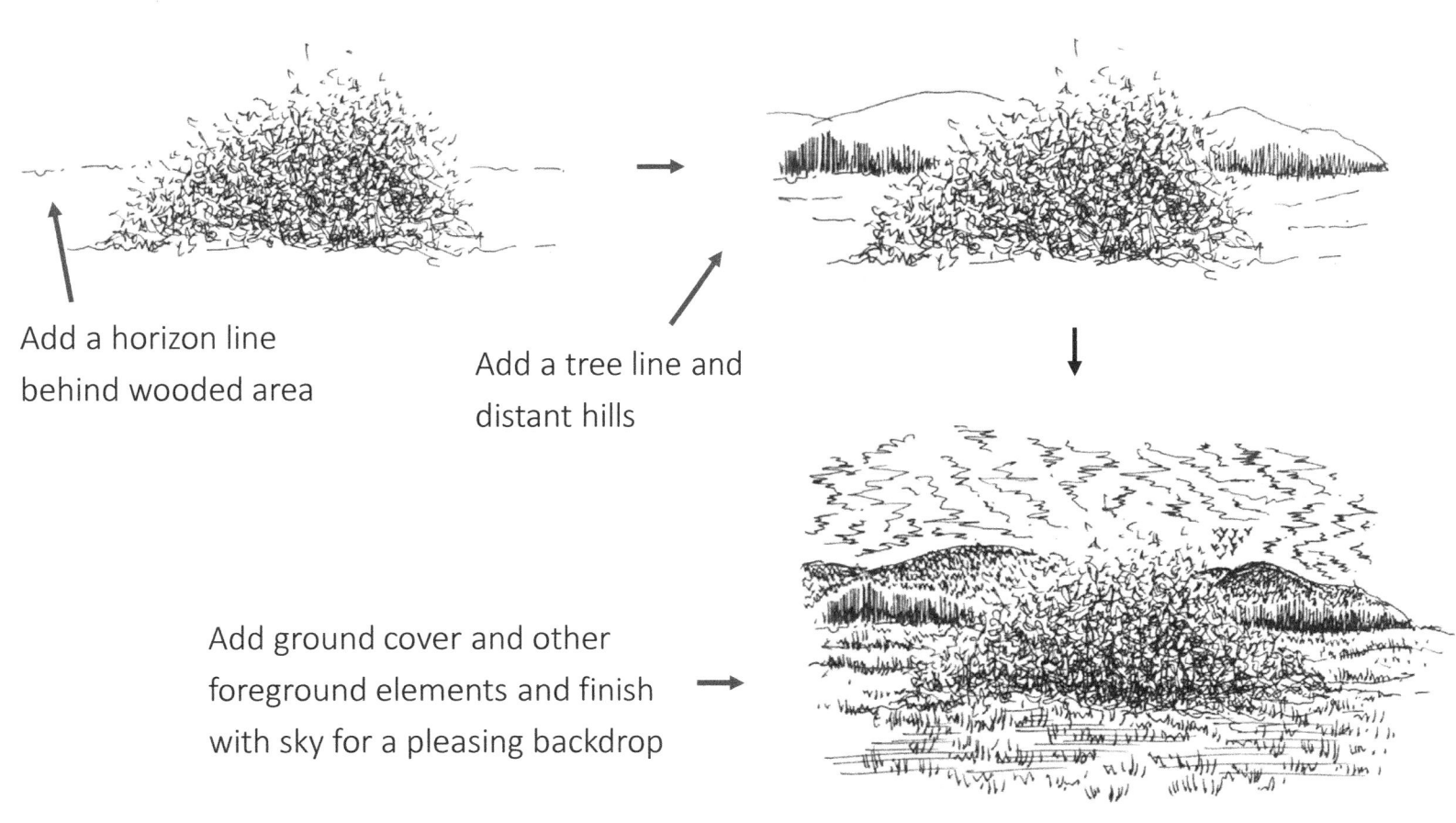

Add a horizon line behind wooded area

Add a tree line and distant hills

Add ground cover and other foreground elements and finish with sky for a pleasing backdrop

Drawing other elements of nature like mountains, sky, stones etc. is covered in other volumes in the series. Please visit **www.pendrawings.me/workbooks** for more information.

Adding Other Elements, Another Example:

A wooded area followed by a backdrop of other trees and a distant hill is also a pleasing composition theme. Other things like a path, stones etc. can be added to create more visual interest. There indeed is no end to such simple pleasing compositions incorporating a wooded area. Try one now.

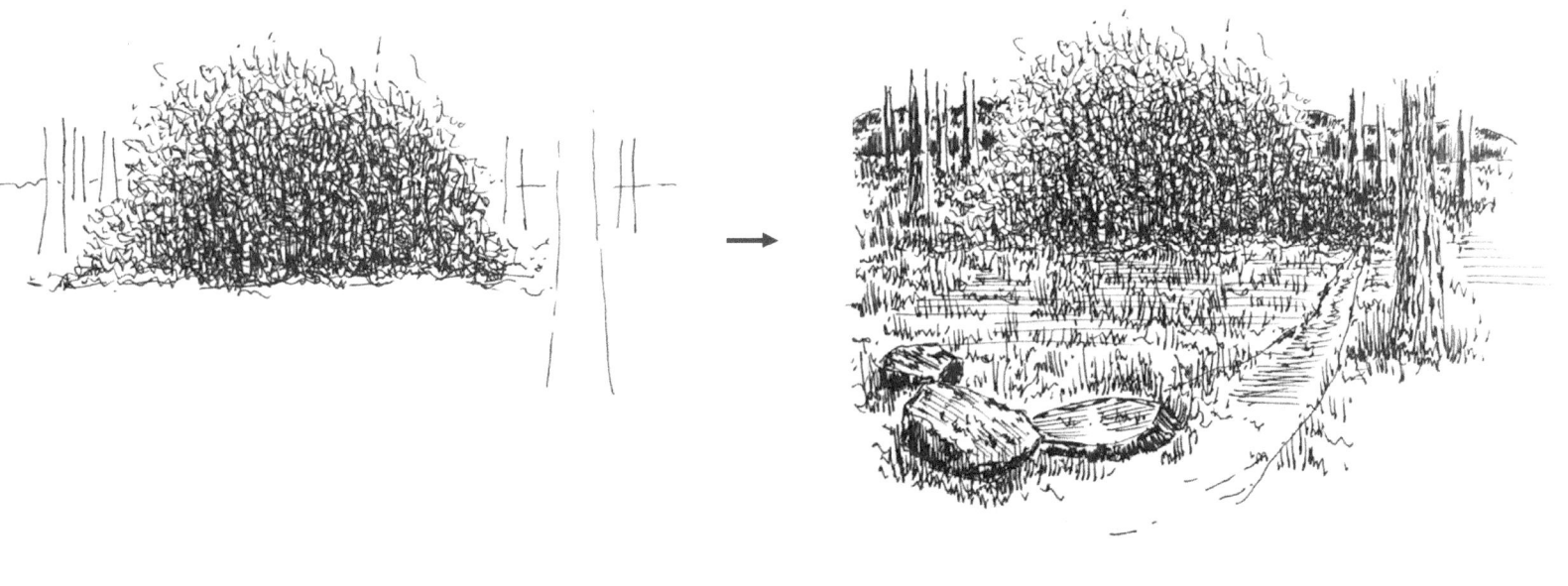

Adding Other Elements, Yet Another Example:

In this example, the left side foliage is receding, i.e. becomes smaller with distance along the path. Most of the examples in the book are drawn facing viewer but same technique can be used to draw them receding in this manner. Combination of receding and non receding foliage like here adds visual appeal to the drawing.

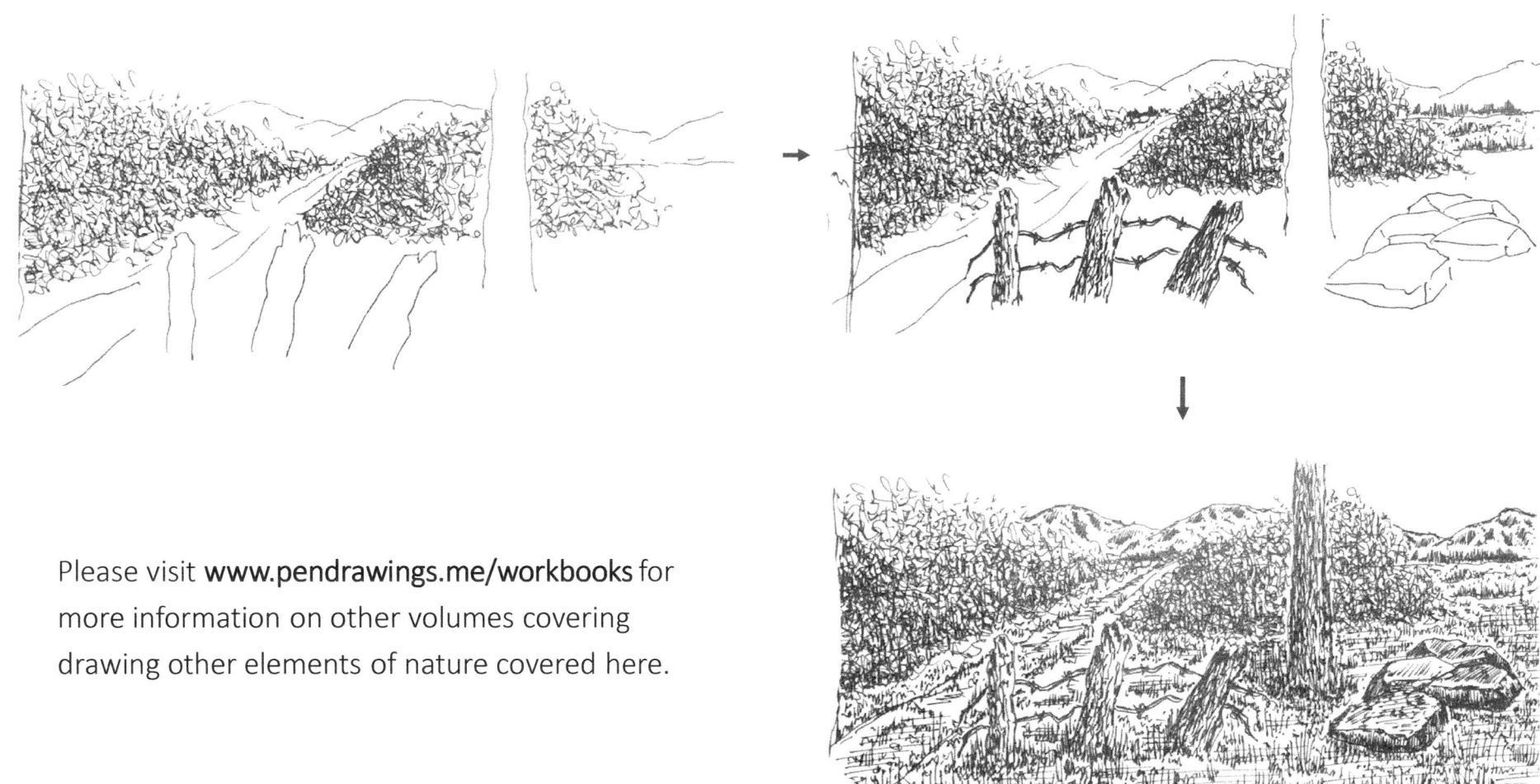

Please visit **www.pendrawings.me/workbooks** for more information on other volumes covering drawing other elements of nature covered here.

Another Example Incorporating Wooded Area:

Trees peeking from a wooded area like in this drawing also gives a pleasing feel. Experiment with such different combinations of shapes, foliage, tree density and positions etc. in your attempts. Great thing with such drawings is that one can be easily drawn from our imagination anytime. Try one now.

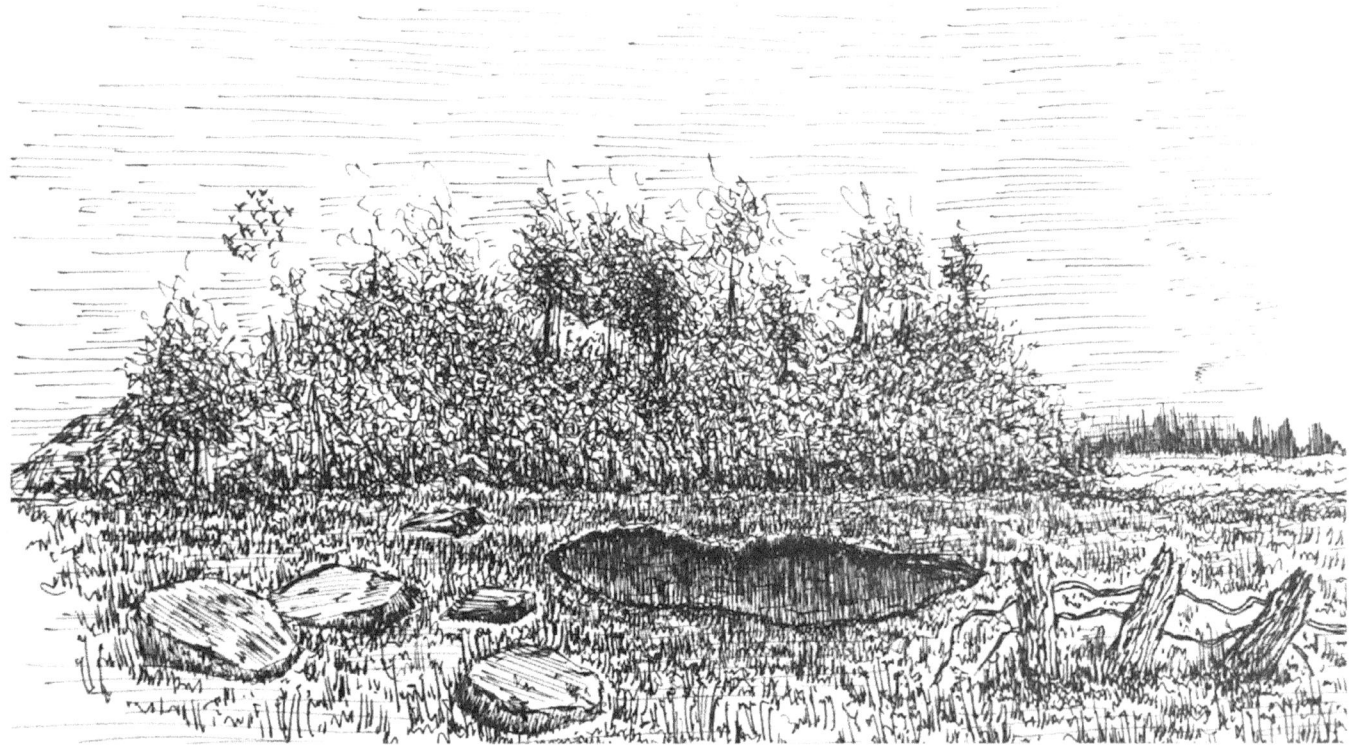

Drawing Wooded Scene with Bigger Vertical Trunks:

In new few techniques, we will learn how to use mature vertical tree trunks as the main elements to create a wooded setting. This creates a wooded setting with more of a 'forest' feel as compared to last few techniques.

In these techniques, receding tree trunks are drawn initially. They are not drawn twisted and overlapping as in techniques before, but in more of straight manner. Resulting drawings using these techniques have more of feel of 'forest' that we are familiar with.

Drawing a Wooded Setting with Trunks:

In this technique, we start by drawing tree trunks at different distance to the viewer. Bigger trunks are closer to the viewer while smaller trunks are closer to the horizon (in background, or away from the viewer).

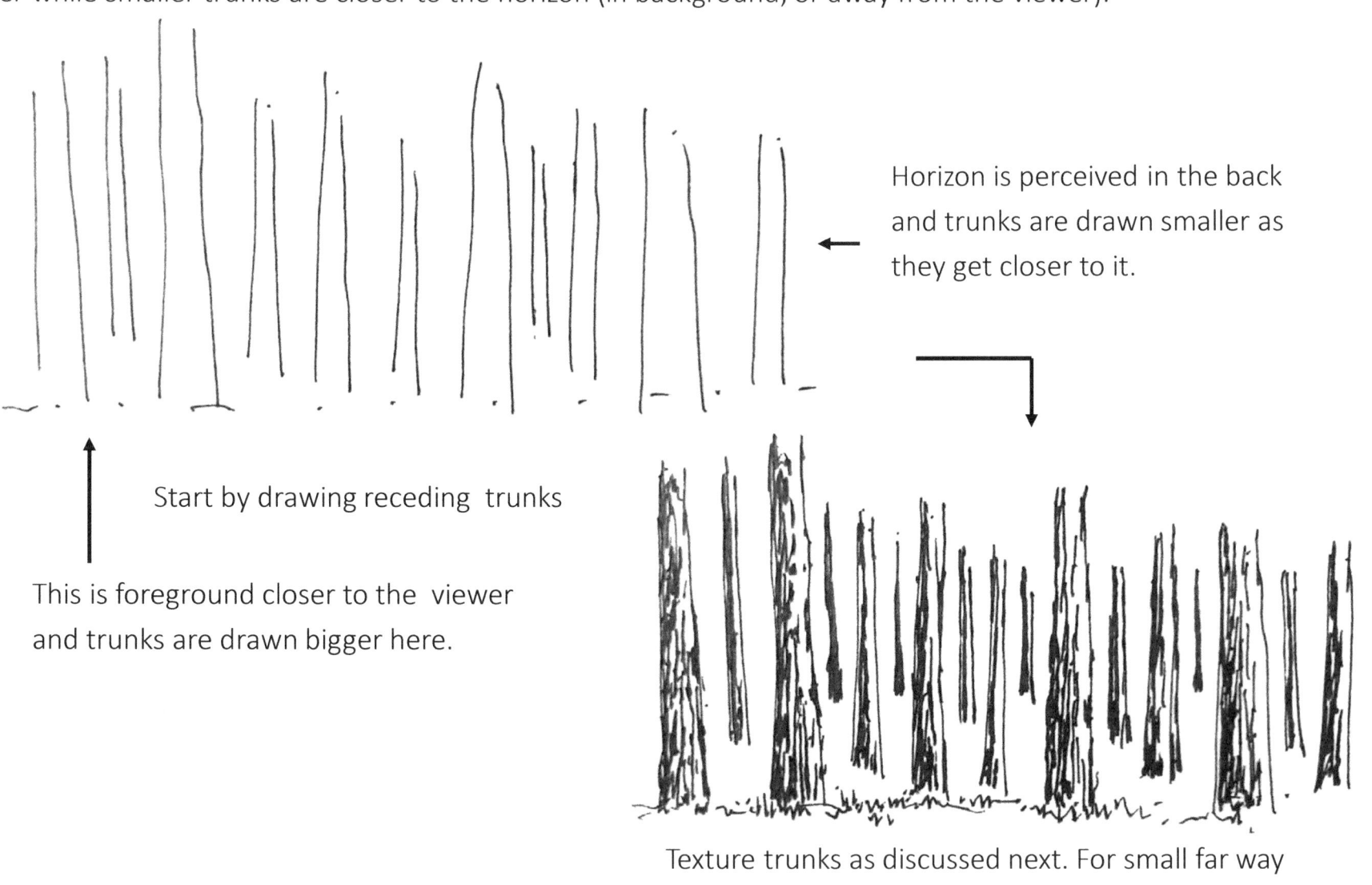

Horizon is perceived in the back and trunks are drawn smaller as they get closer to it.

Start by drawing receding trunks

This is foreground closer to the viewer and trunks are drawn bigger here.

Texture trunks as discussed next. For small far way trunks, use 2 tone technique as discussed earlier.

Texturing Tree Trunk:

Texturing trunk is important part of this technique. Following stroke and steps can be used to effectively texture and bring out feel of trunk. Texturing trunks is discussed in detail in other volumes in the series.

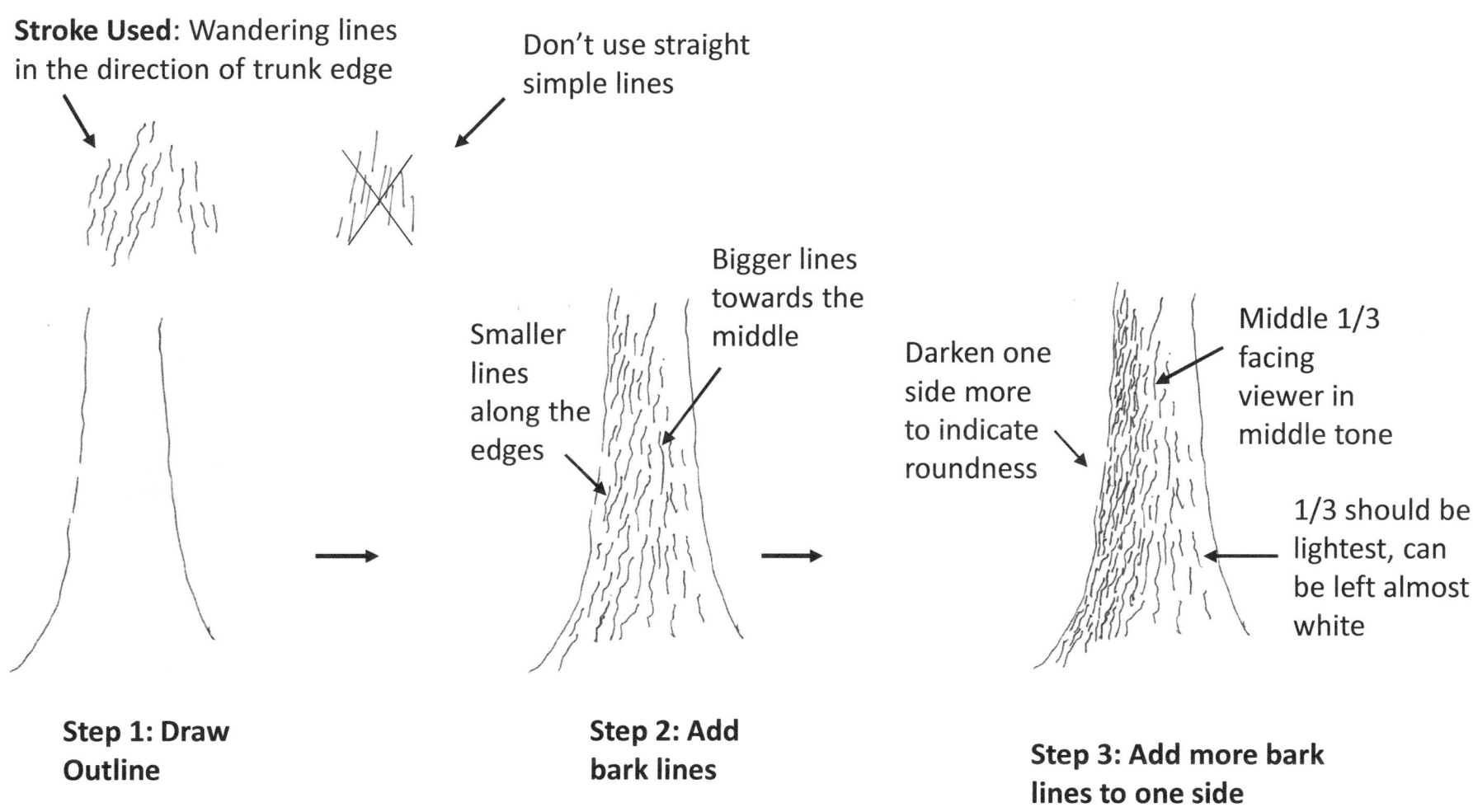

Texturing Tree Trunk:

After adding bark stroke, tapered crevices and edge irregularities can be added as shown below to further bring out the feel of trunk.

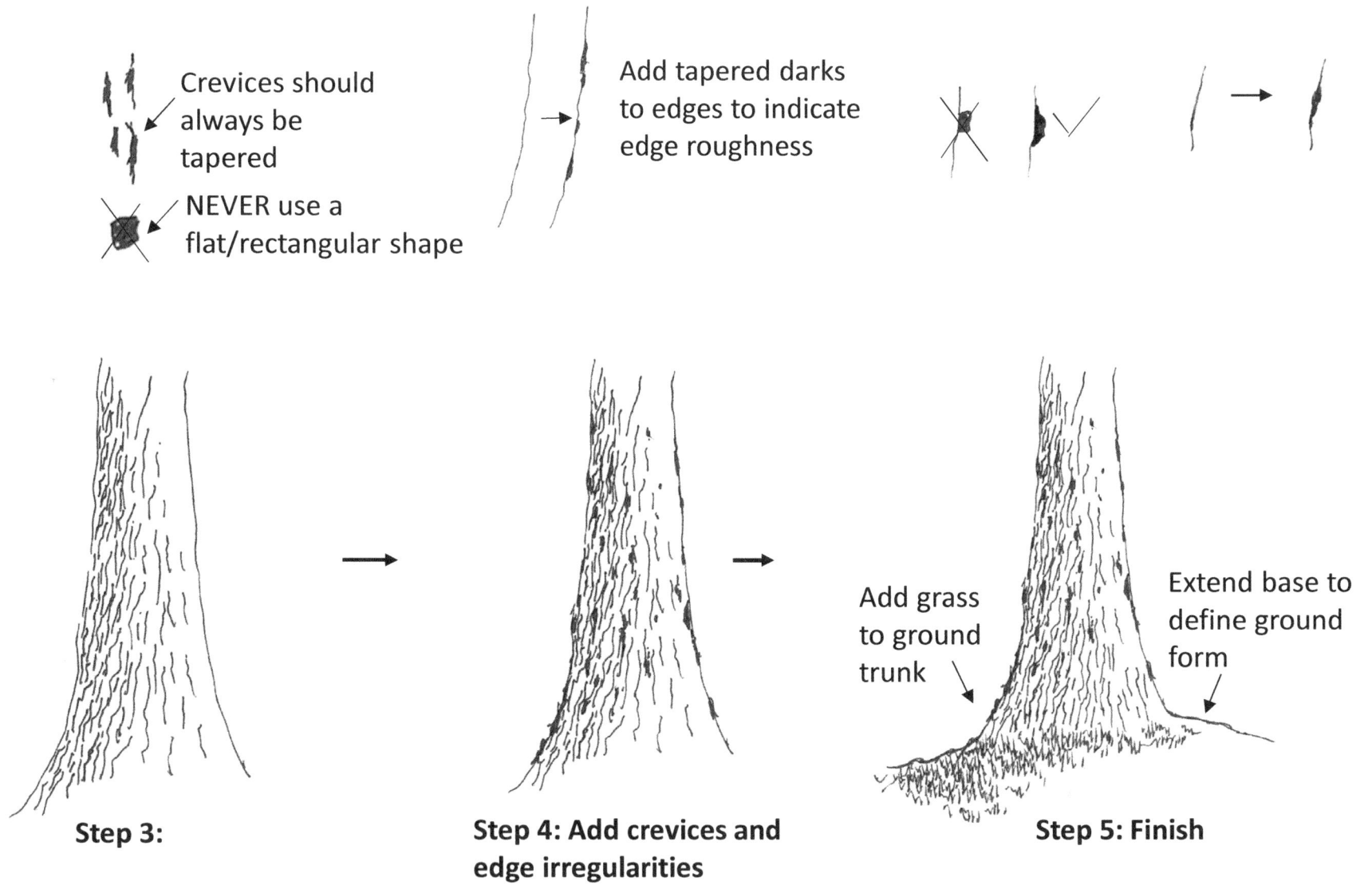

Crevices should always be tapered

NEVER use a flat/rectangular shape

Add tapered darks to edges to indicate edge roughness

Step 3:

Step 4: Add crevices and edge irregularities

Add grass to ground trunk

Extend base to define ground form

Step 5: Finish

Drawing a Wooded Setting with Trunks, Continued:

Add a backdrop of angular parallel lines as discussed before.

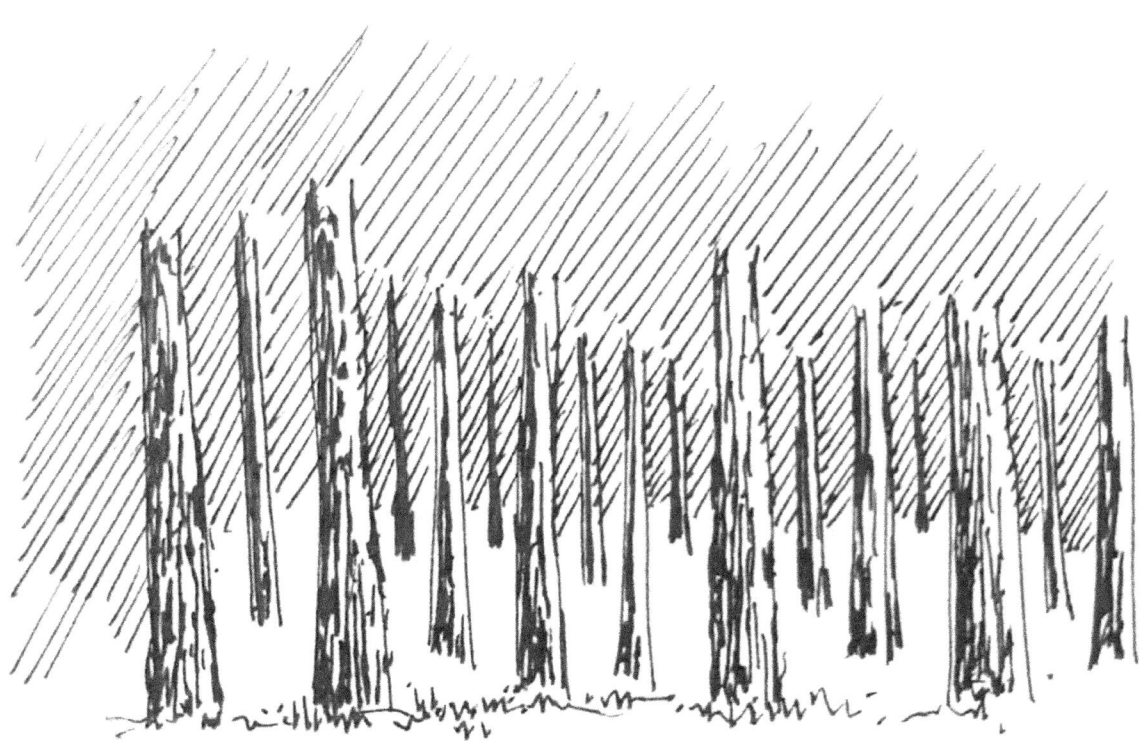

Drawing a Wooded Setting with Trunks, Completed:

Add grass as ground cover to finish. Trunks further out can be draw as solid tapered dark as well to further add depth. Here we haven't added any foliage but foliage can be added between trunks as well. This is discussed next.

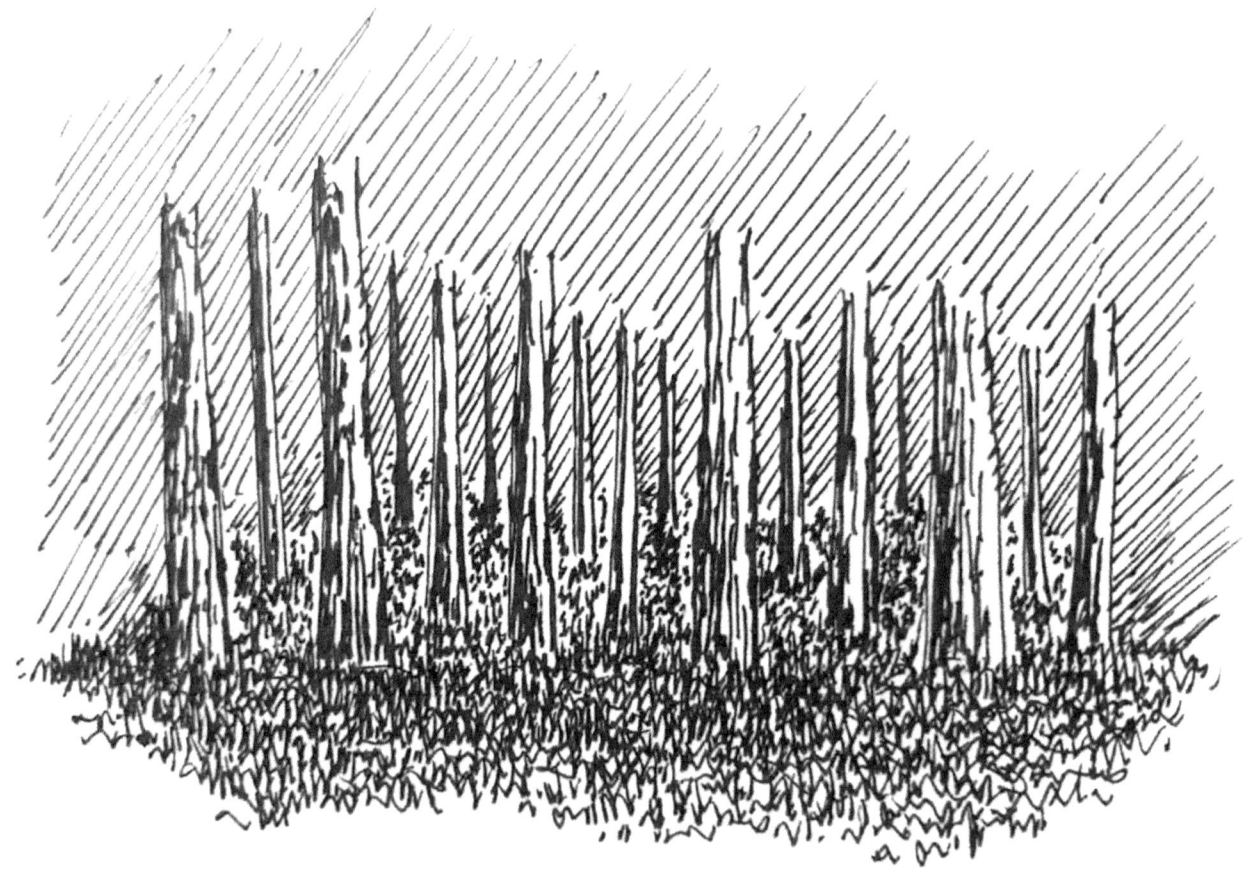

This is a basic receding trunk drawing that is pleasant in itself and is also the basis for drawing a 'forest' setting. By using different combination of sizes and placement of trunks, such pleasing drawing can be done from imagination anytime. Try one now.

Moving Horizon:

Moving the horizon line changes the elevation of distant plain with respect to the viewer as seen below. Choose the right placement of horizon line based on the effect you intent to have in our drawing.

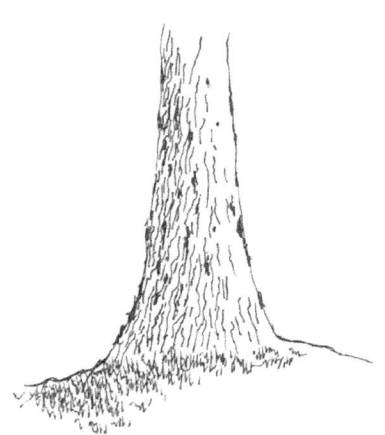
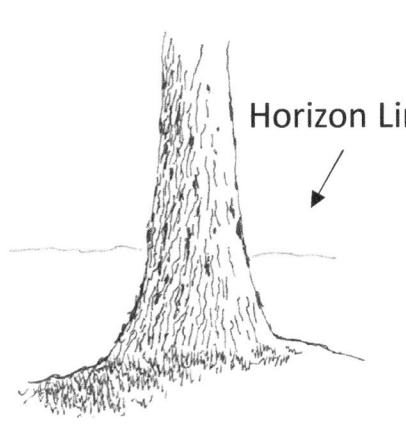
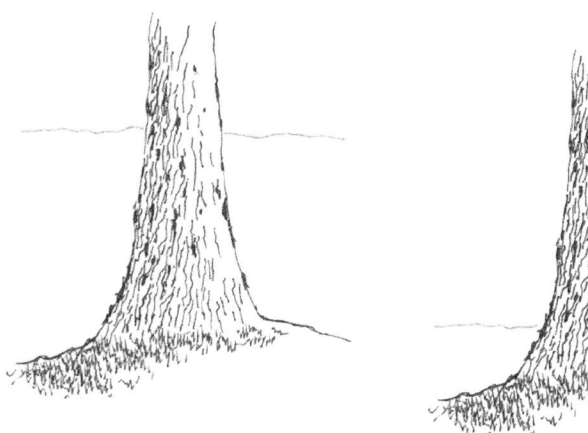

No explicit horizon line. We imagine 'far out' in the distance.

Putting the horizon line makes the far out explicit.

Moving horizon up or down changes how we are looking at the distance. Moving Horizon up makes it feel as it we are looking up from below while moving it down does the reverse.

Moving Horizon, Some Examples:

Notice how greater perception of distance is obtained by moving horizon line further away from foreground. Experiment with different position of horizon line to see its effect on the feel it evokes in final drawing.

Horizon line is moved back below making our eyes travel more distance.

Horizon line is closer to foreground below which moves horizon lower with less perceived distance.

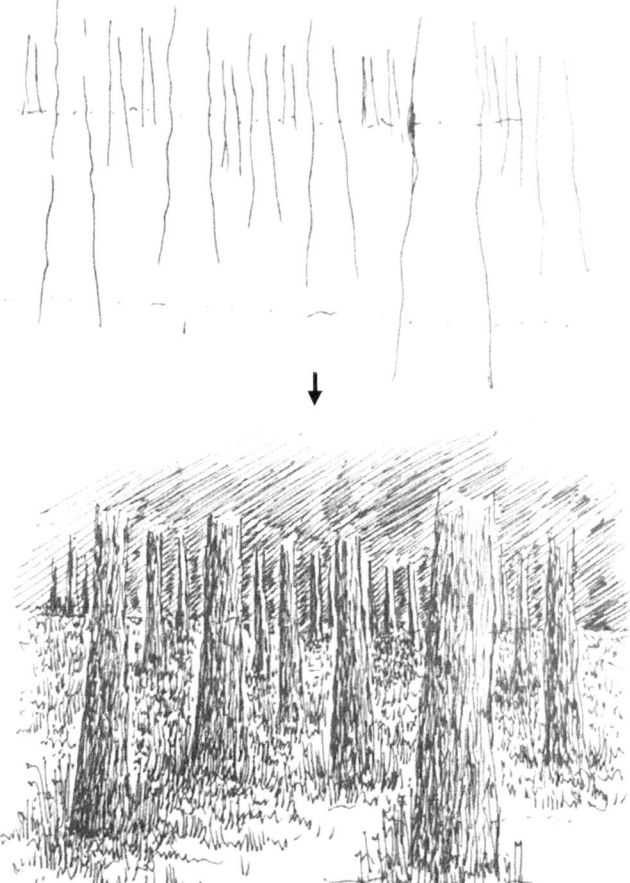

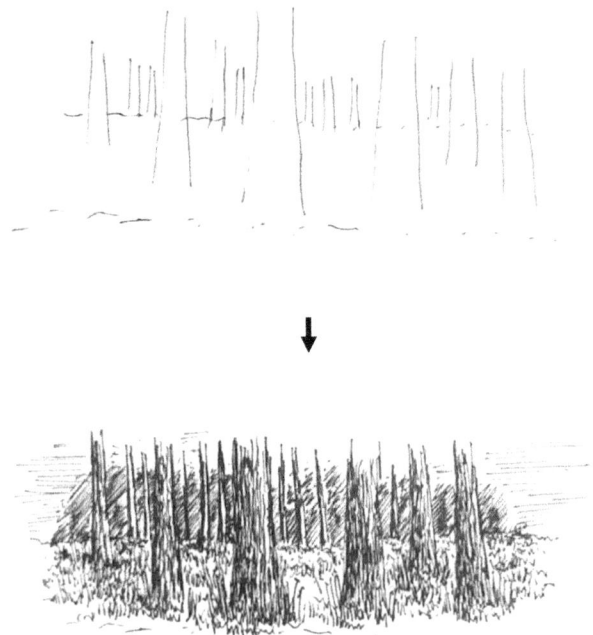

Drawing a Wooded Setting with Trunks and Foliage:

This technique is similar to previous one where receding trunks are drawn first. But here, foliage is added between the trunks to give a different feel for the wooded setting.

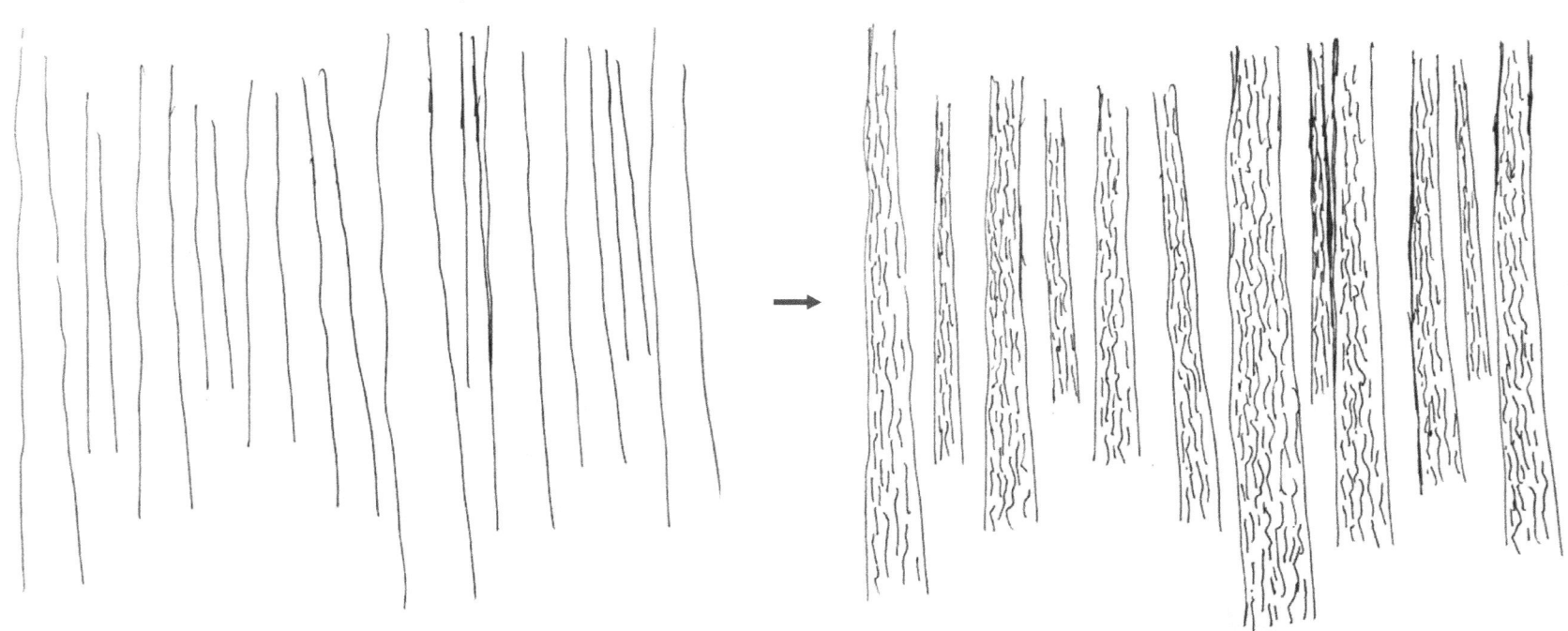

Start by drawing receding trunks outline and texturing them as before. Notice that horizon is not explicitly put down in the beginning but is settled on in the end based on how the drawing proceeds.

Drawing a Wooded Setting with Trunks and Foliage, Continued:

Choose the density of foliage and trunks per your liking. By using different combination of foliage and trunks, different feel is obtained in the drawing.

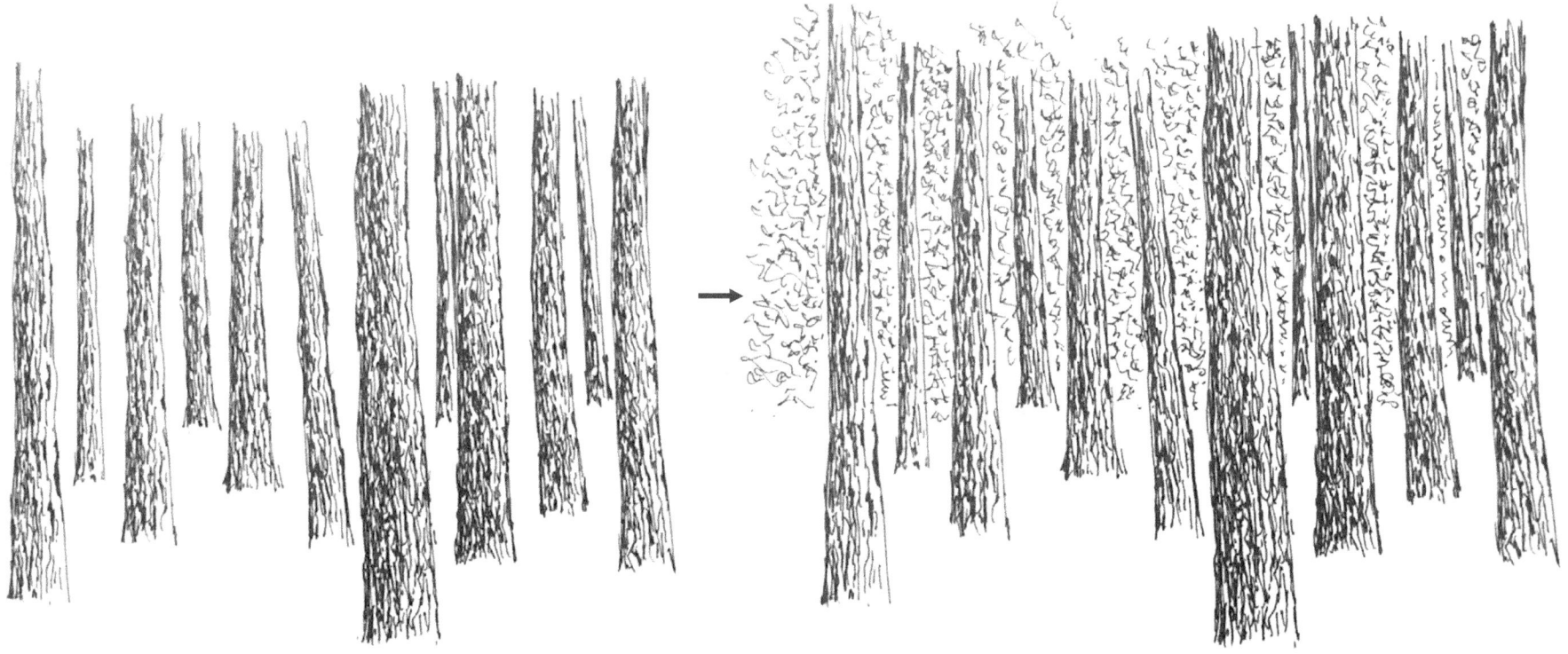

Foliage is added between the Trunks. Different foliage strokes as discussed before can be used.

Drawing a Wooded Setting with Trunks and Foliage, Continued:

Trunks are rounded and ground is added next. This starts to give a feel of forest. Notice that lack of tonal variation in the foliage makes it appear flat. This is fixed next.

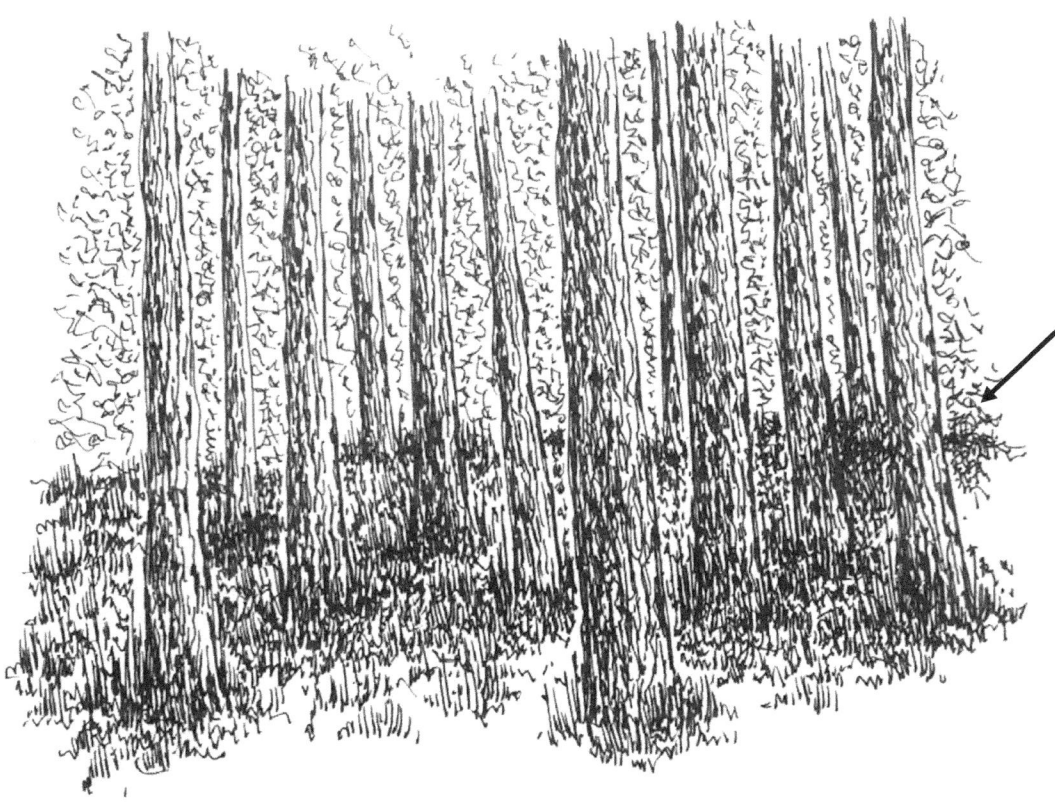

Horizon is established by darkening it more. There should be a tonal difference between horizon area, background foliage and ground cover for them to stand out.

Grounding trunks and adding ground cover is very important. This is discussed in detail later.

Drawing a Wooded Setting with Trunks and Foliage, Completed:

Tonal variation is added to the foliage by darkening it irregularly in some places. This gives perception of depth and makes the drawing more appealing.

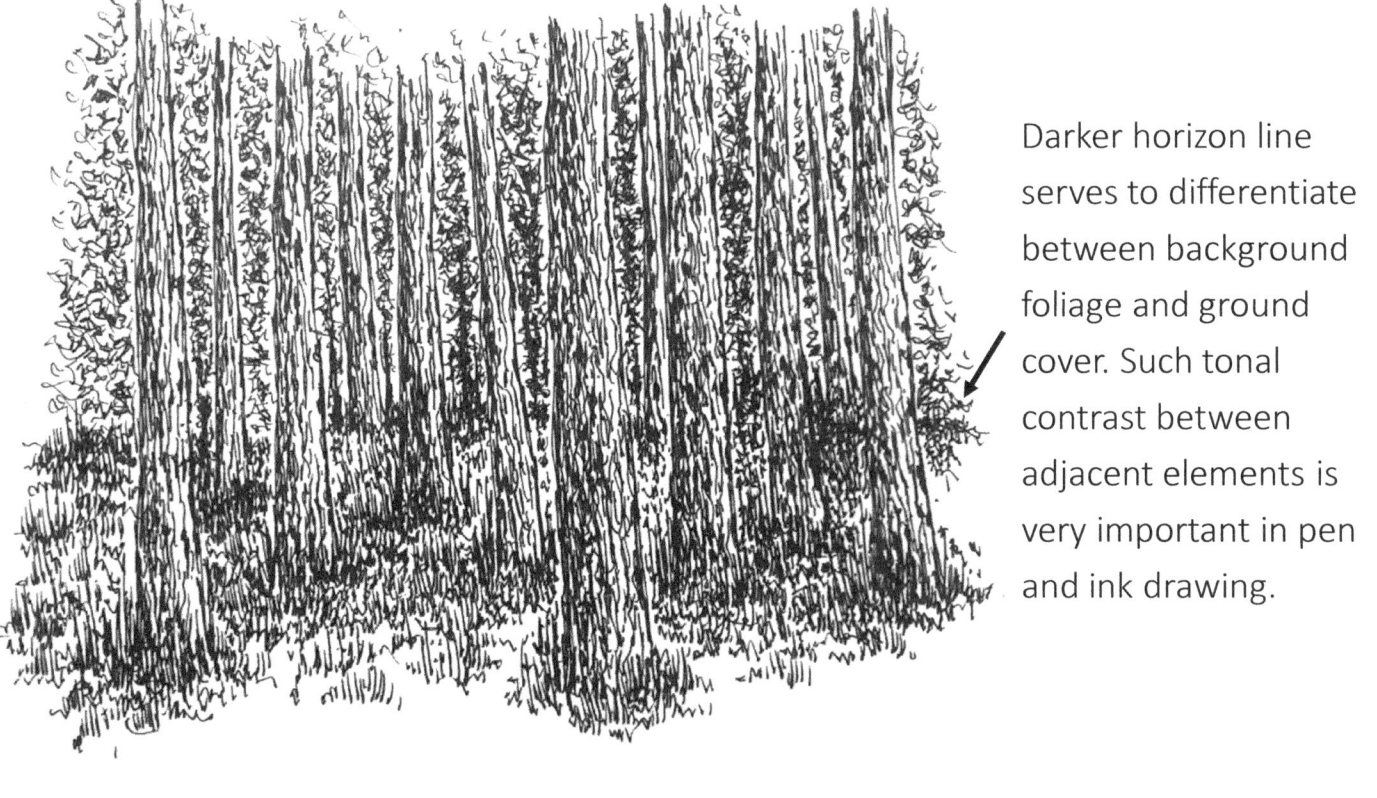

Darker horizon line serves to differentiate between background foliage and ground cover. Such tonal contrast between adjacent elements is very important in pen and ink drawing.

Alternate Approach to Drawing a Wooded Setting with Trunks and Foliage:

In the previous approach, foliage was added between the trunks at the end giving it a particular feel. In another approach, scattered foliage masses can be drawn initially and trunks drawn partially hidden behind them. This gives more perception of depth and gives a different feel to the setting.

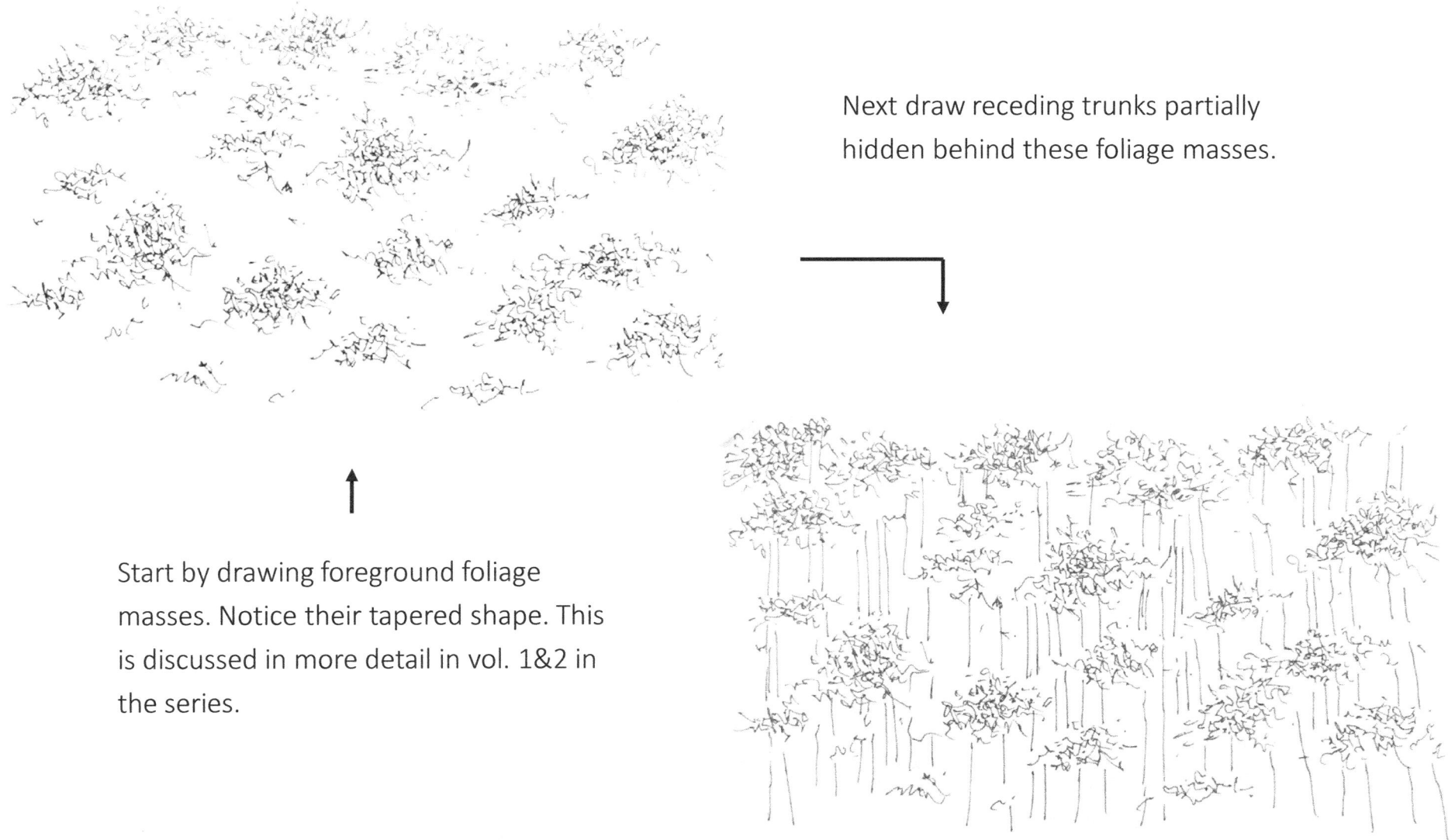

Next draw receding trunks partially hidden behind these foliage masses.

Start by drawing foreground foliage masses. Notice their tapered shape. This is discussed in more detail in vol. 1&2 in the series.

Drawing a Wooded Setting with Trunks and Foliage, Finished:

Here angular parallel lines are used to indicate background foliage with darker tone. This establishes a nice contrast between the foreground and background foliage and gives perception of depth. Also grass is textured with less tone than background tone and this clearly establishes a change from ground cover to background foliage .

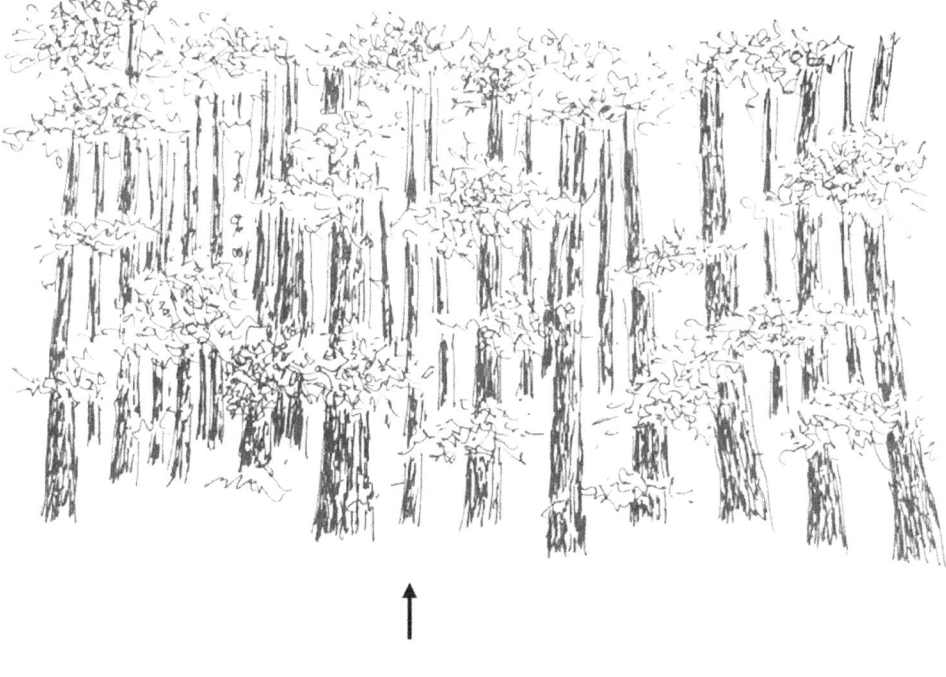

Texture trunks as discussed before.

Add background foliage and ground cover.
Background is textured darker to make it stand out from ground cover.

Comparative Study:

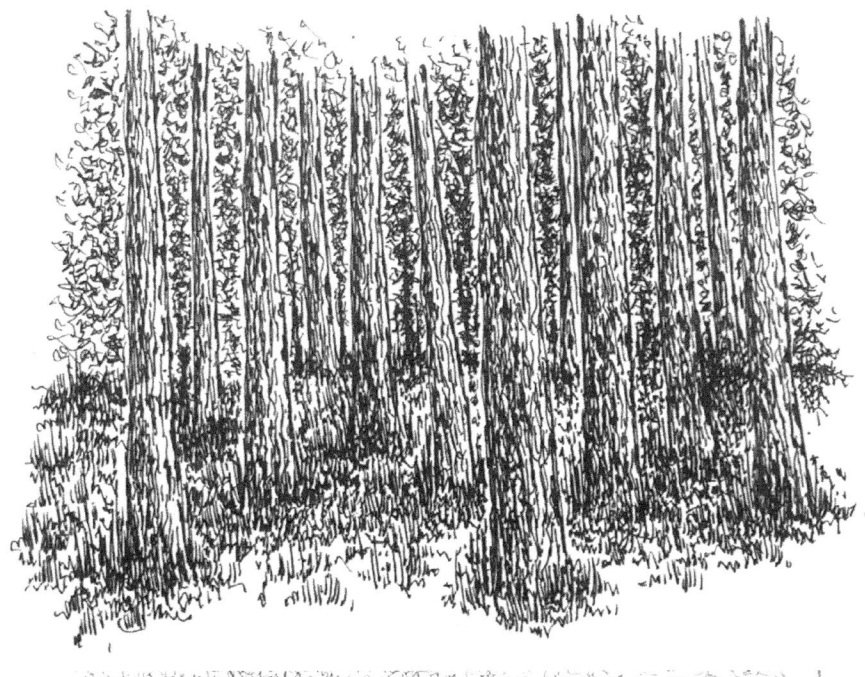

Here is a comparative study of different ways of drawing foliage. Two drawing we saw before. Third on bottom left is drawn using the last technique but with low contrast between foreground and background. Notice the different feel in these drawings. There indeed is no limit to how different variations on these technique can be used to draw a pleasant wooded setting. Try one now.

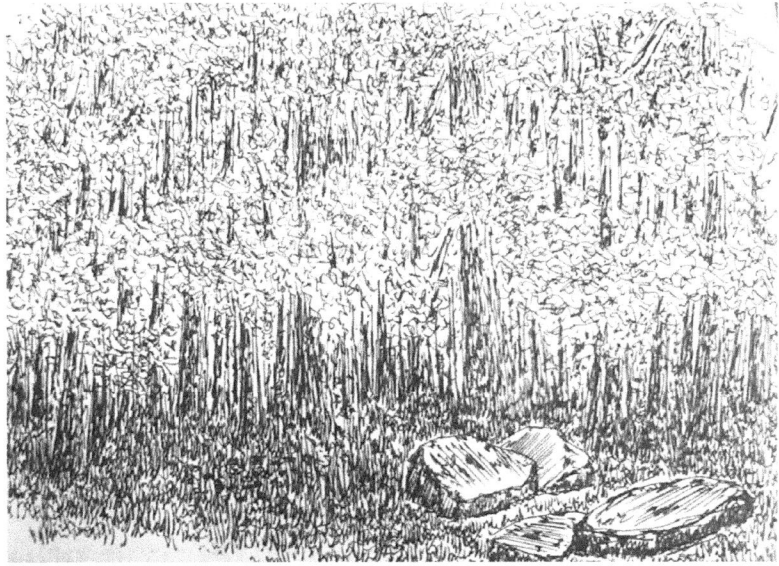

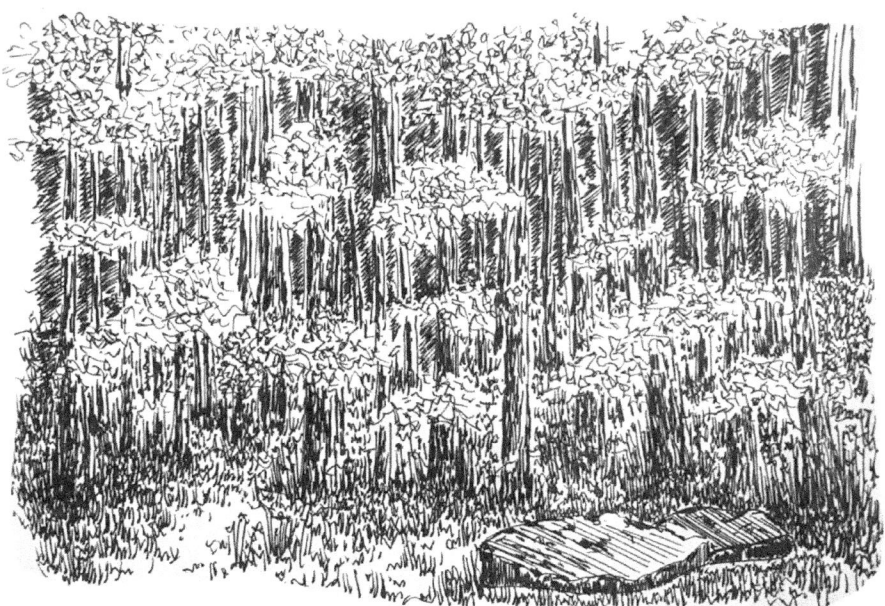

Small Size Drawings:

This technique can be used to draw quick, smaller sized pleasing forest setting in between your break. With variation on following steps, you can draw a new drawing from your imagination any time.

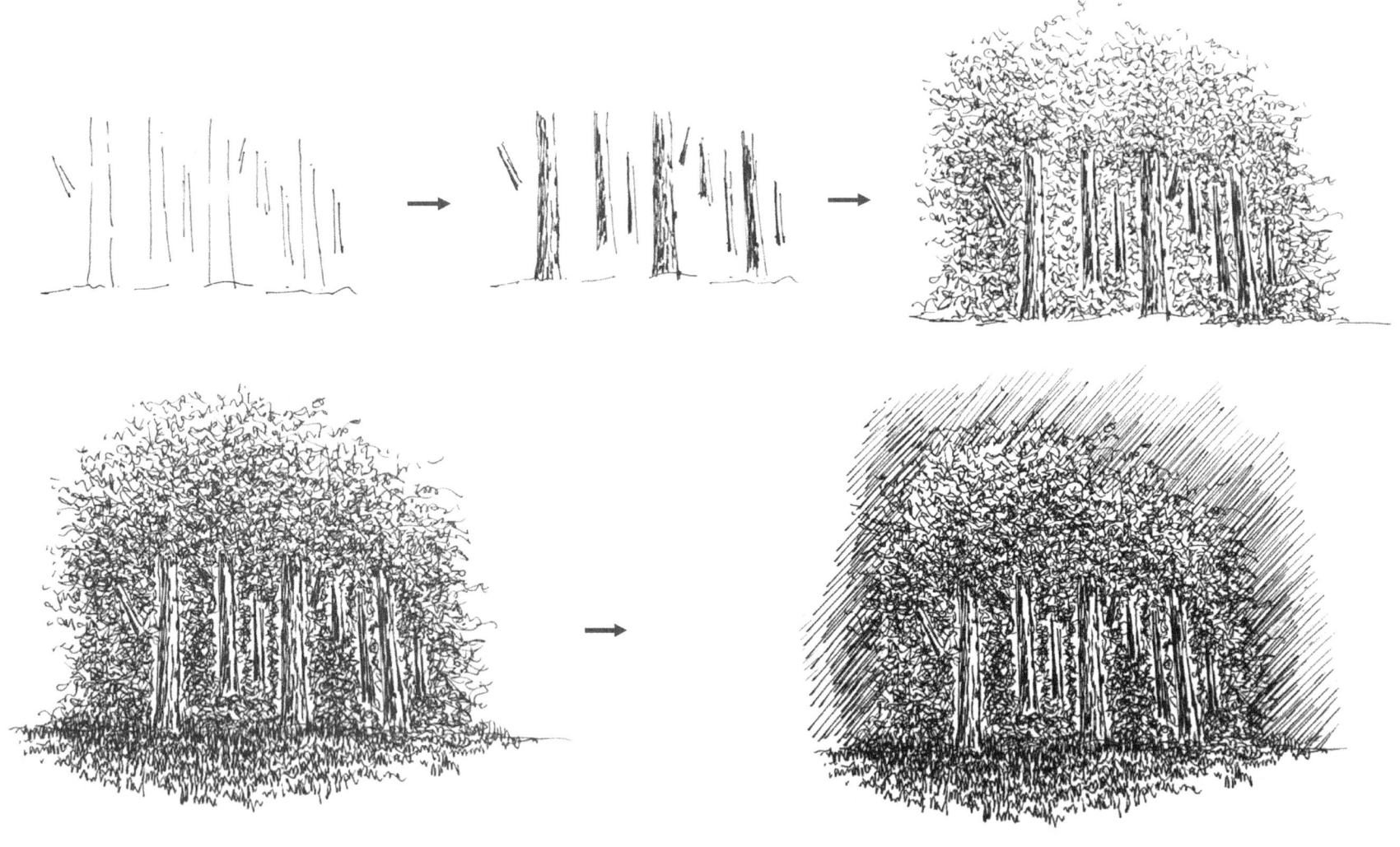

More Examples:

There really is no limit to the type of forest and wooded areas that can be drawn in this manner. Here are some more examples. Try one of your own now.

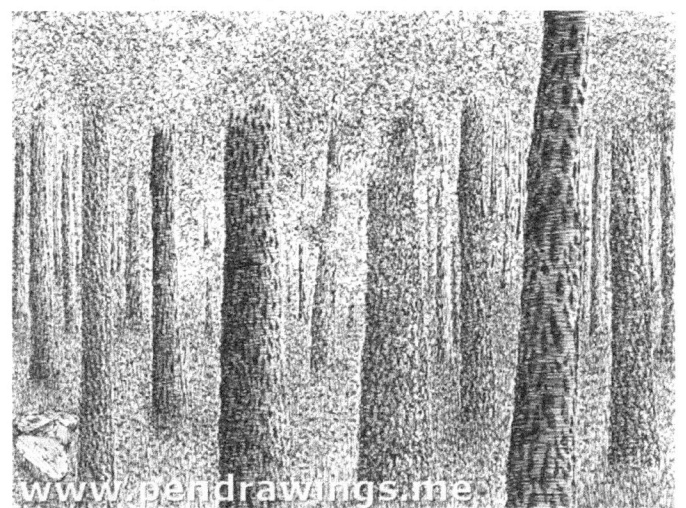
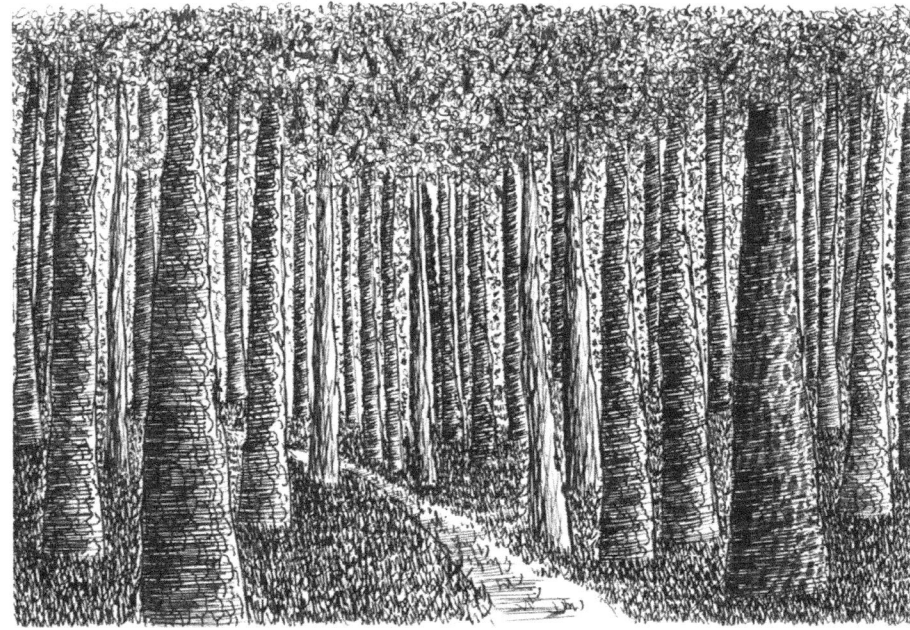
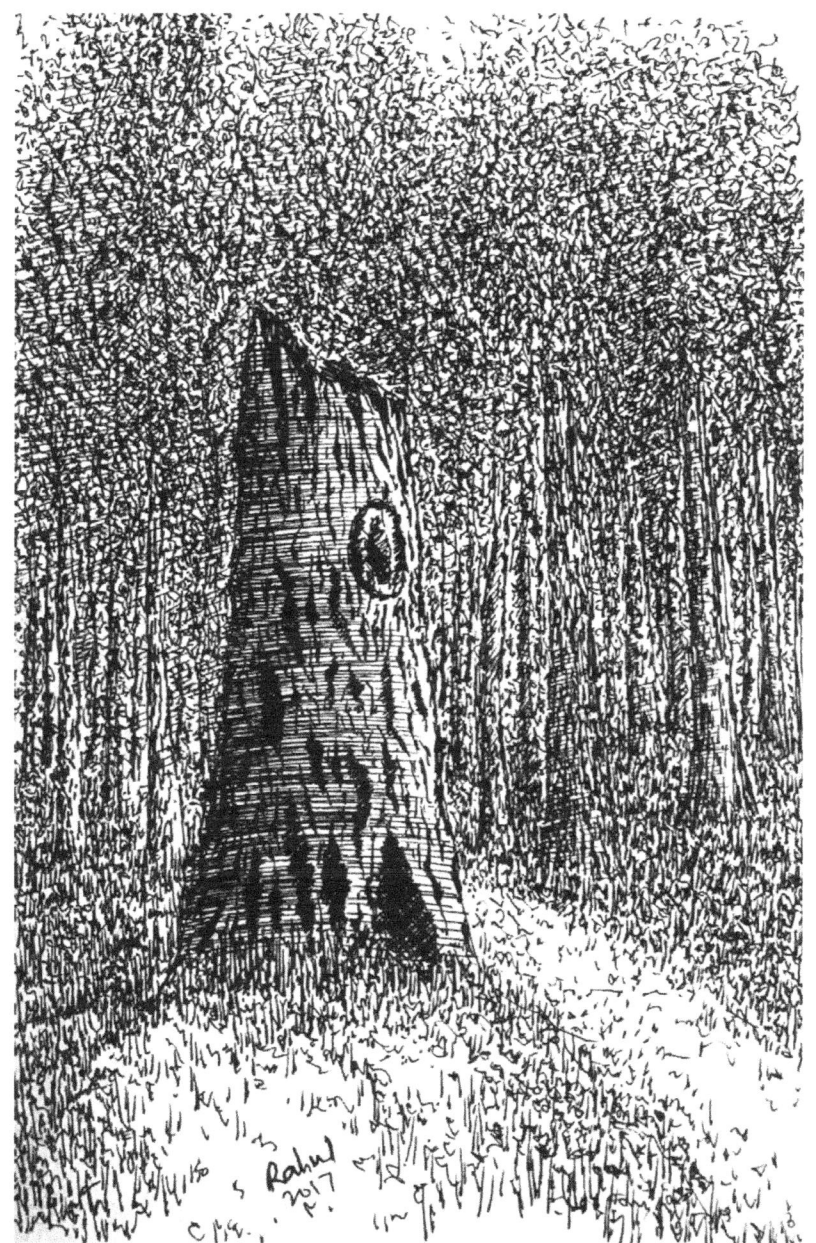

Wooded Area with Angular Parallel Lines:

Next we look at techniques for drawing a wooded area with just angular parallel lines. These lines were used earlier to provide a backdrop to a wooded area but we will next see how such lines can be used to also draw a wooded area. Wooded areas drawn in this manner have a 'hazy' appearance. Such wooded areas can be used as a background to other elements in front. In these compositions, the focus is on front elements with the wooded area providing a pleasing backdrop. But wooded areas with this technique can be the primary focus as well especially with a backdrop of mountains or hills.

It takes practice to be able to draw such parallel lines. Carry a small pocket sketch book with you and practice drawing these lines whenever you get a chance. The key aspect is that lines should be 'more or less' equidistant from each other. In the beginning you might struggle to achieve it with your lines sloping off and mixing with each other, but be persistent. It is much more difficult to draw longer parallel lines than to draw shorter parallel lines. So, focus your effort on getting shorter parallel lines (1.5 to 2 inches) right initially.

As you get comfortable with drawing shorter parallel lines, gradually attempt longer lines. If you feel frustrated, then take a break and try again. Parallel lines are the basis for adding tones in pen and ink drawing and as such are a fundamental aspect of drawing with pen and ink. Spending time learning to draw them will help you in drawing other elements of nature as well.

Drawing a Wooded Setting with Angular Parallel Lines:

In this technique, angular parallel lines are used to draw a wooded scene. The key aspect of the technique is to use multiple layers of parallel lines to create different tones and convey a feel of foliage and trees.

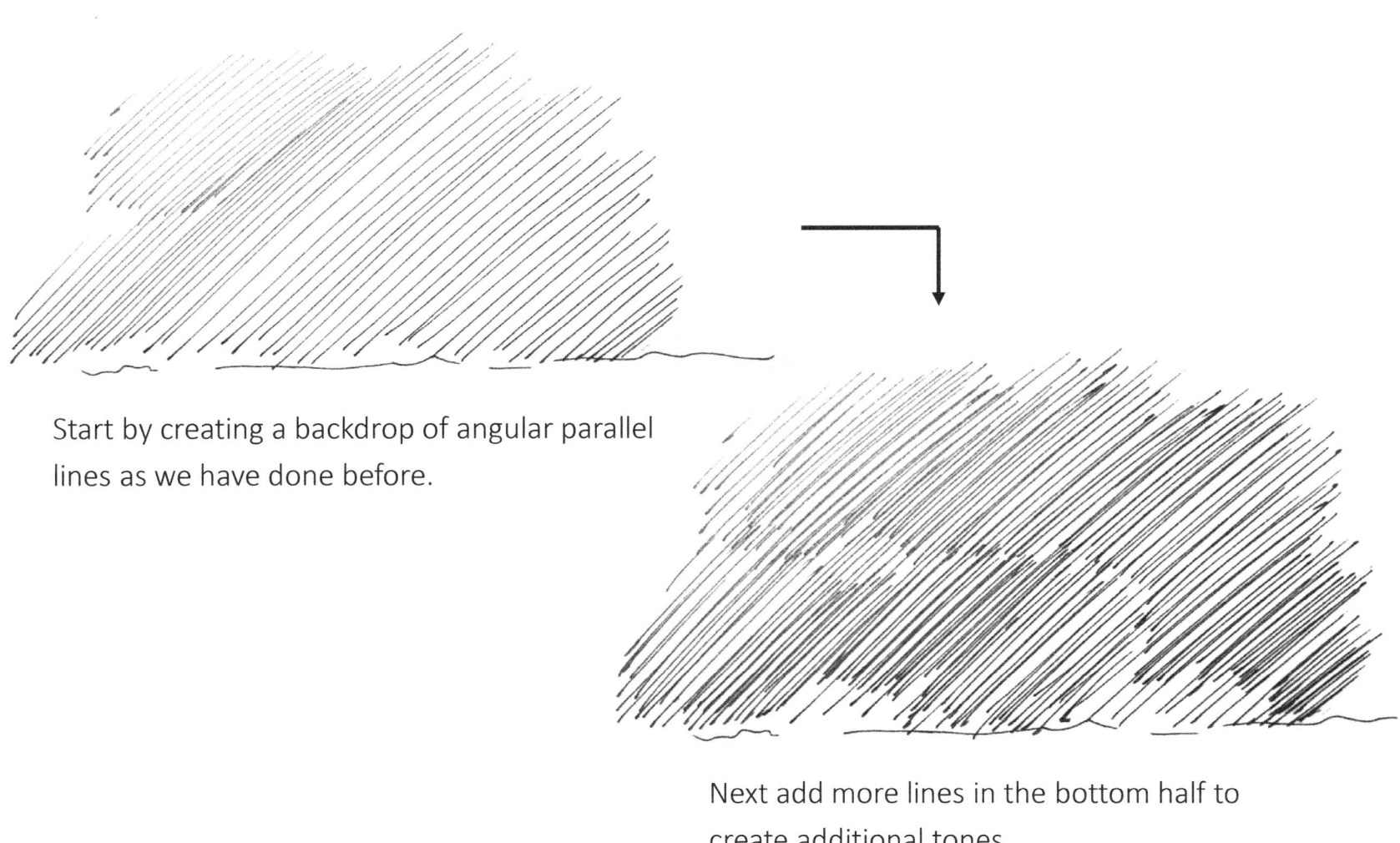

Start by creating a backdrop of angular parallel lines as we have done before.

Next add more lines in the bottom half to create additional tones.

Drawing a Wooded Setting with Angular Parallel Lines, Continued:

Key to success behind this technique is to use additional set of lines in an irregular manner to give feel of foliage and trees.

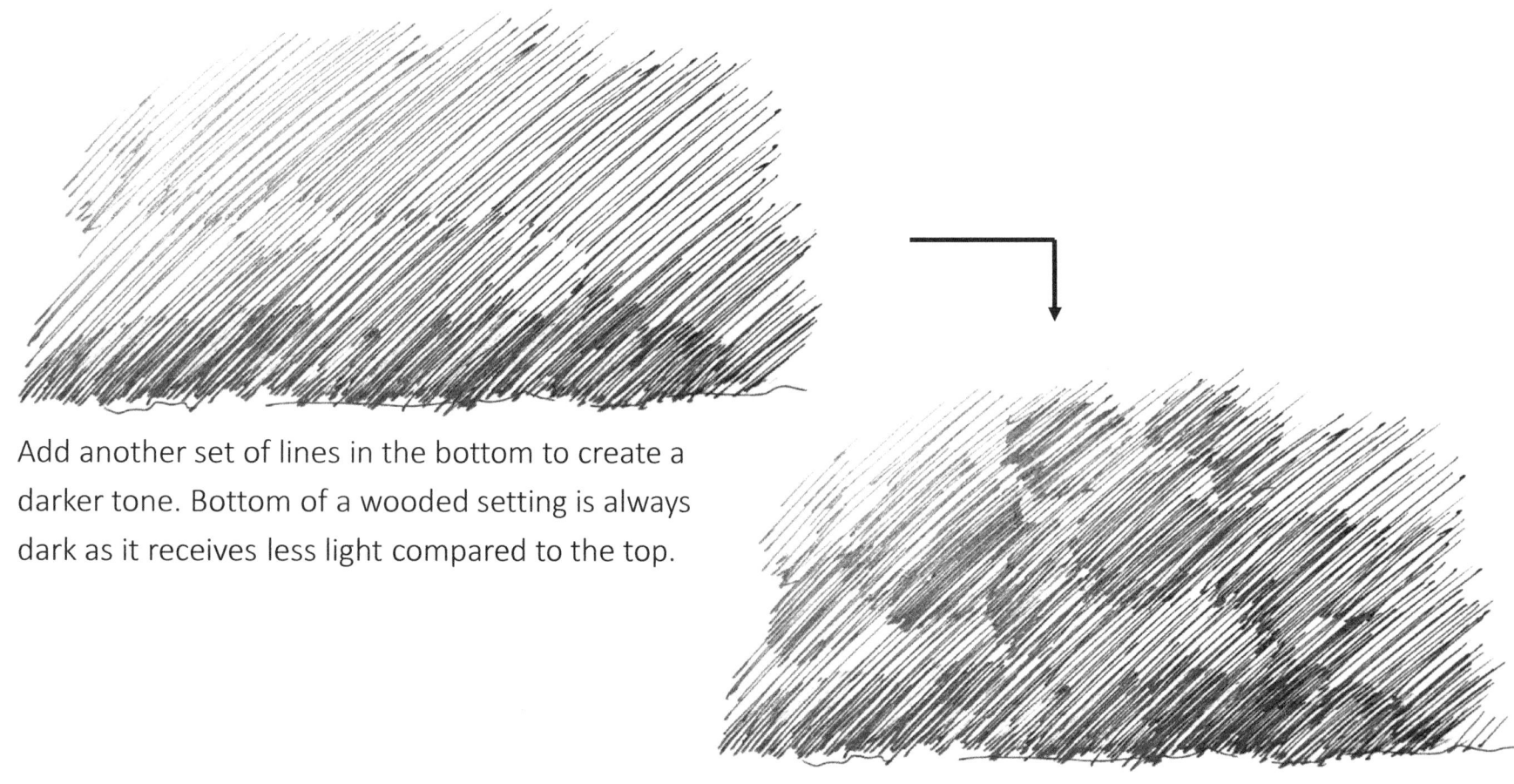

Add another set of lines in the bottom to create a darker tone. Bottom of a wooded setting is always dark as it receives less light compared to the top.

Add another layer in the shape of ovals at the top to indicate tree foliage. Make sure it is irregular as shown above to bring out the desired feel.

Drawing a Wooded Setting with Angular Parallel Lines, Continued:

Level of darker tones used in a drawing is a matter of personal preference. Darker tones convey an intense and sometimes foreboding feeling. What is most important is that there is a tonal difference between different areas of the drawing to indicate form of trees, foliage etc. and to bring out the depth.

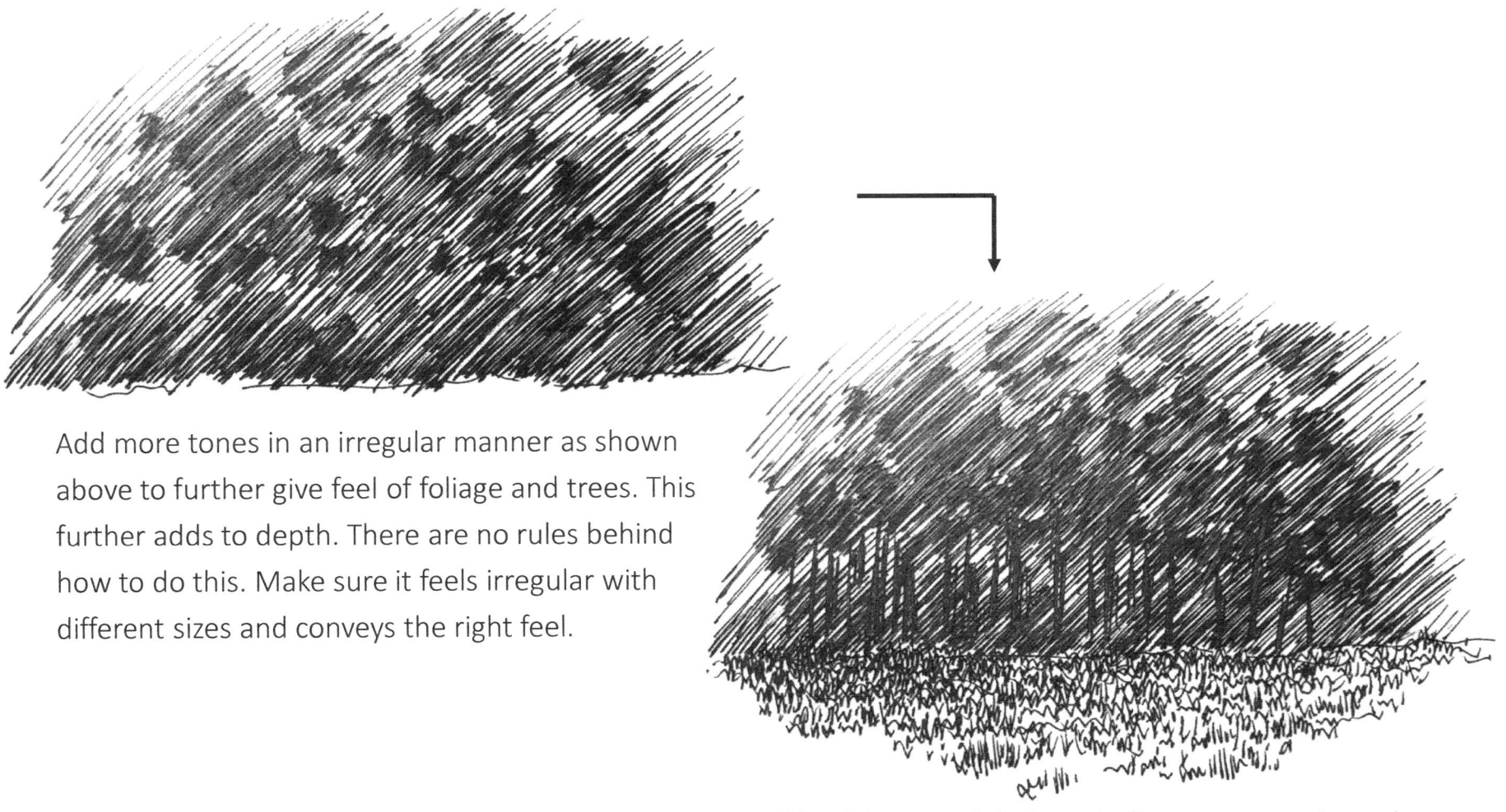

Add more tones in an irregular manner as shown above to further give feel of foliage and trees. This further adds to depth. There are no rules behind how to do this. Make sure it feels irregular with different sizes and conveys the right feel.

Add solid tapered darks to indicate tree trunks and add grass to finish the drawing.

How to Add Tones:

The main idea behind this technique is to give feel of foliage mass using angular parallel lines. This means that additional tone should be added in the shape of tapered foliage mass. Following figure shows the .typical shapes that can be used. Drawing foliage mass is discussed in more detail in other volumes in the series.

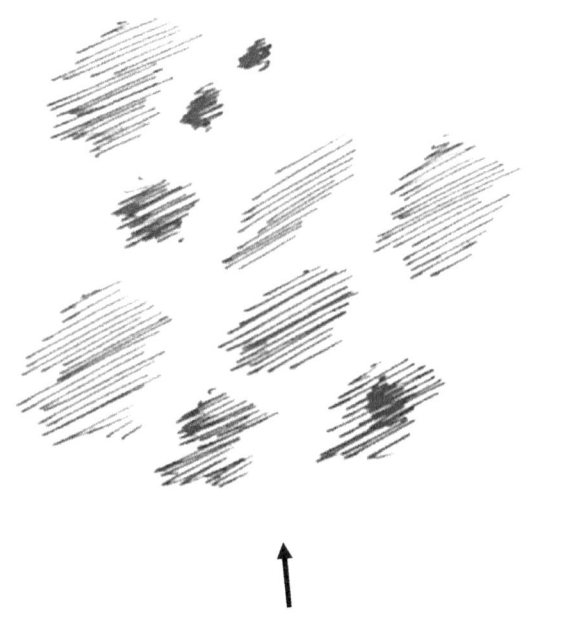

These are the typical shapes to use in this technique to add tone for foliage masses. They are tapered with an overall oval shape. Never use rectangular shape for foliage mass.

Following example of drawing a tree shows how to add them in layers. Start with bigger shapes and successively add smaller darker shapes to get the desired feel.

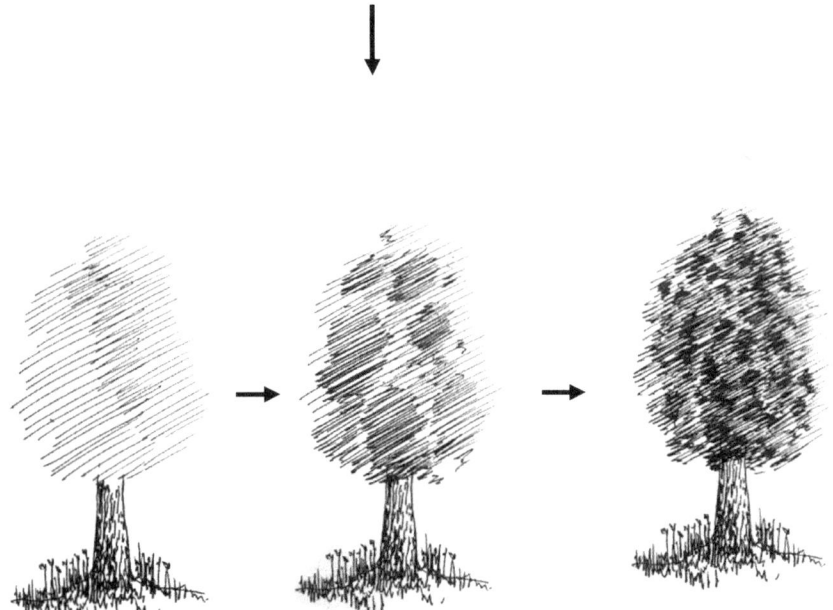

For more information visit www.pendrawings.me/getstarted

Drawing a Wooded Setting with Angular Parallel Lines, More Examples:

Following are some more examples of this technique. This is a very versatile technique and as seen in examples below, by changing the shape, density and manner of use of parallel lines, wooded areas with very different feel can be drawn.

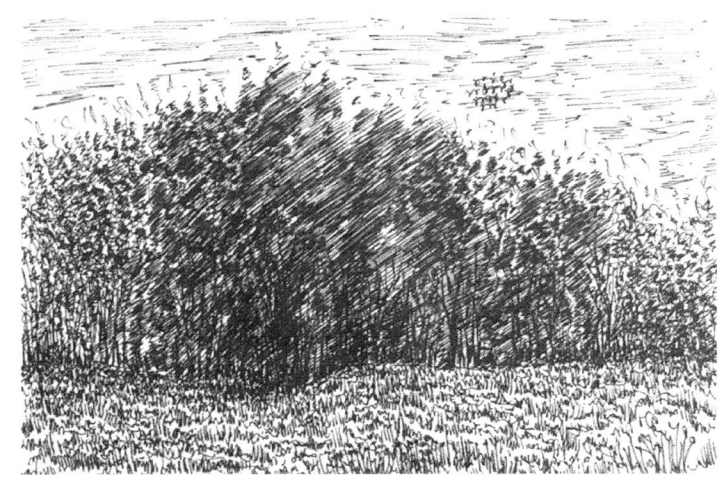

This technique can also be combined with earlier techniques (use of explicit foliage) to further add interest in the drawing. There really is no limit to such fun drawings you can do from your imagination. Try one now.

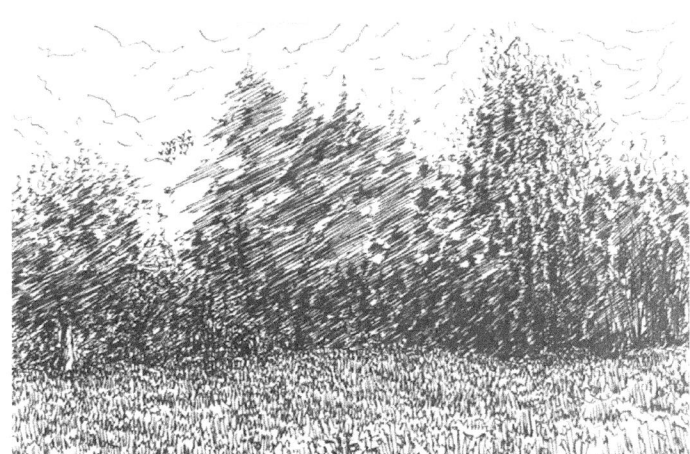

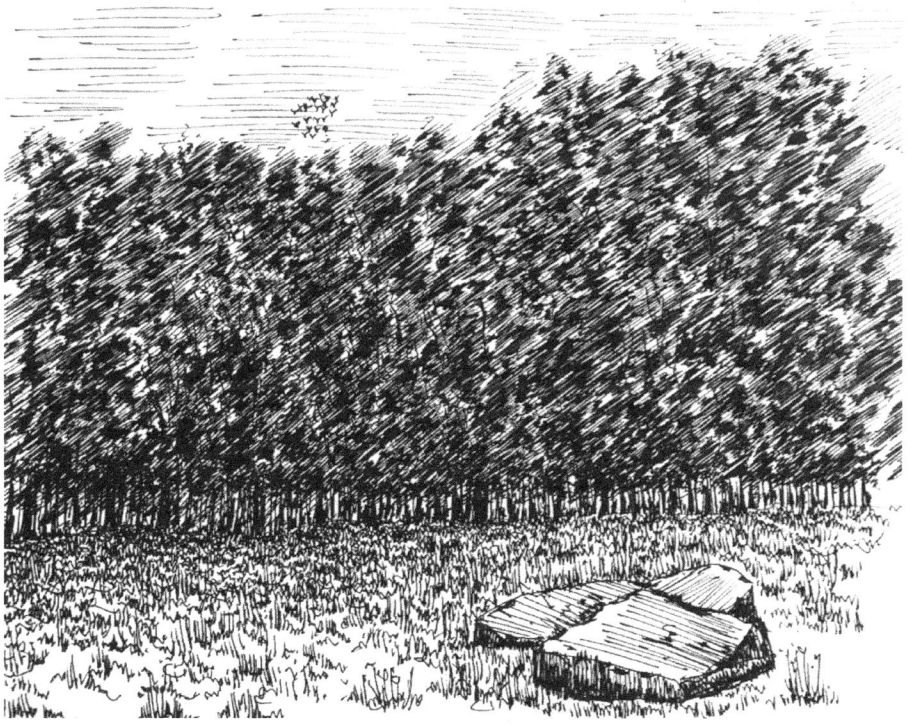

Examples of Drawing a Wooded Setting with Angular Parallel Lines:

In the following examples, this technique is used at a smaller size to provide distant backdrop with other foreground elements. Such small simple landscapes are always fun to do and can be quickly done in between your breaks. Try one now.

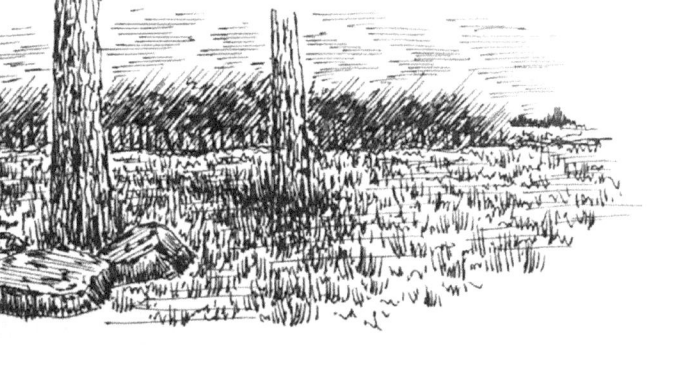

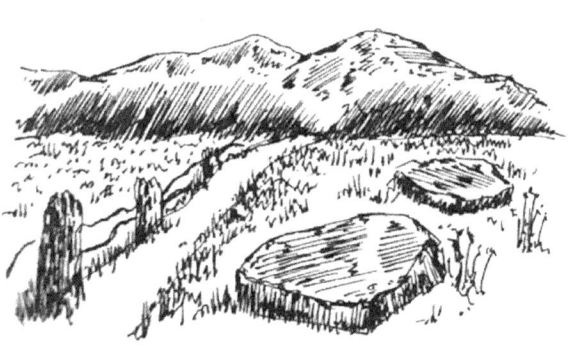

This is the real size of this drawing. Carry a pocket sketch book and attempt such fun drawings in between your breaks.

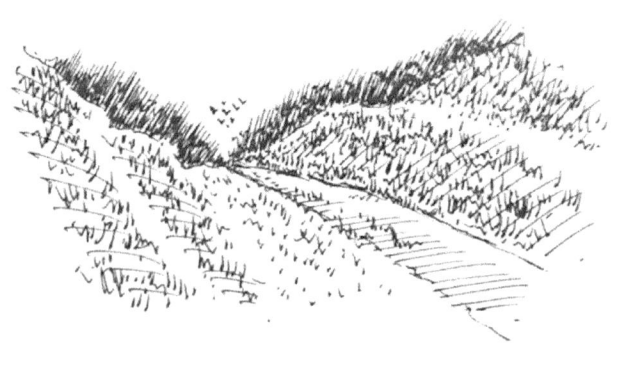

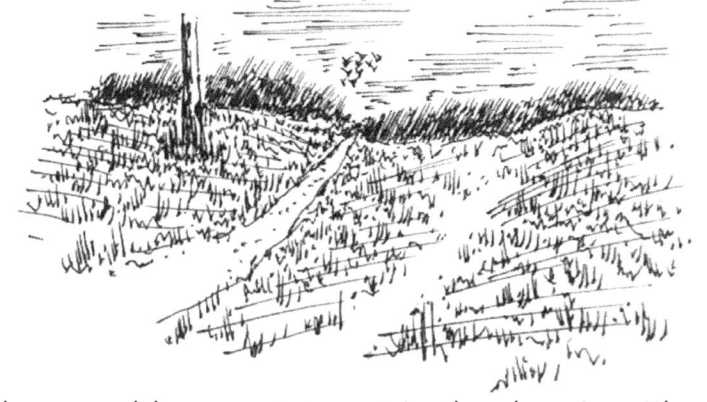

Instead of flat distant wooded area, such distant shapes adds more Interest in the drawing. These are discussed in detail next.

Using Interesting Distant Forms:

Instead of a flat distant contour, it is usually more visually appealing to have more interesting distant forms to add more interest in the drawing. A simple composition is to use a .'U' shape distant form and then add surface definitions to it. This is illustrated below.

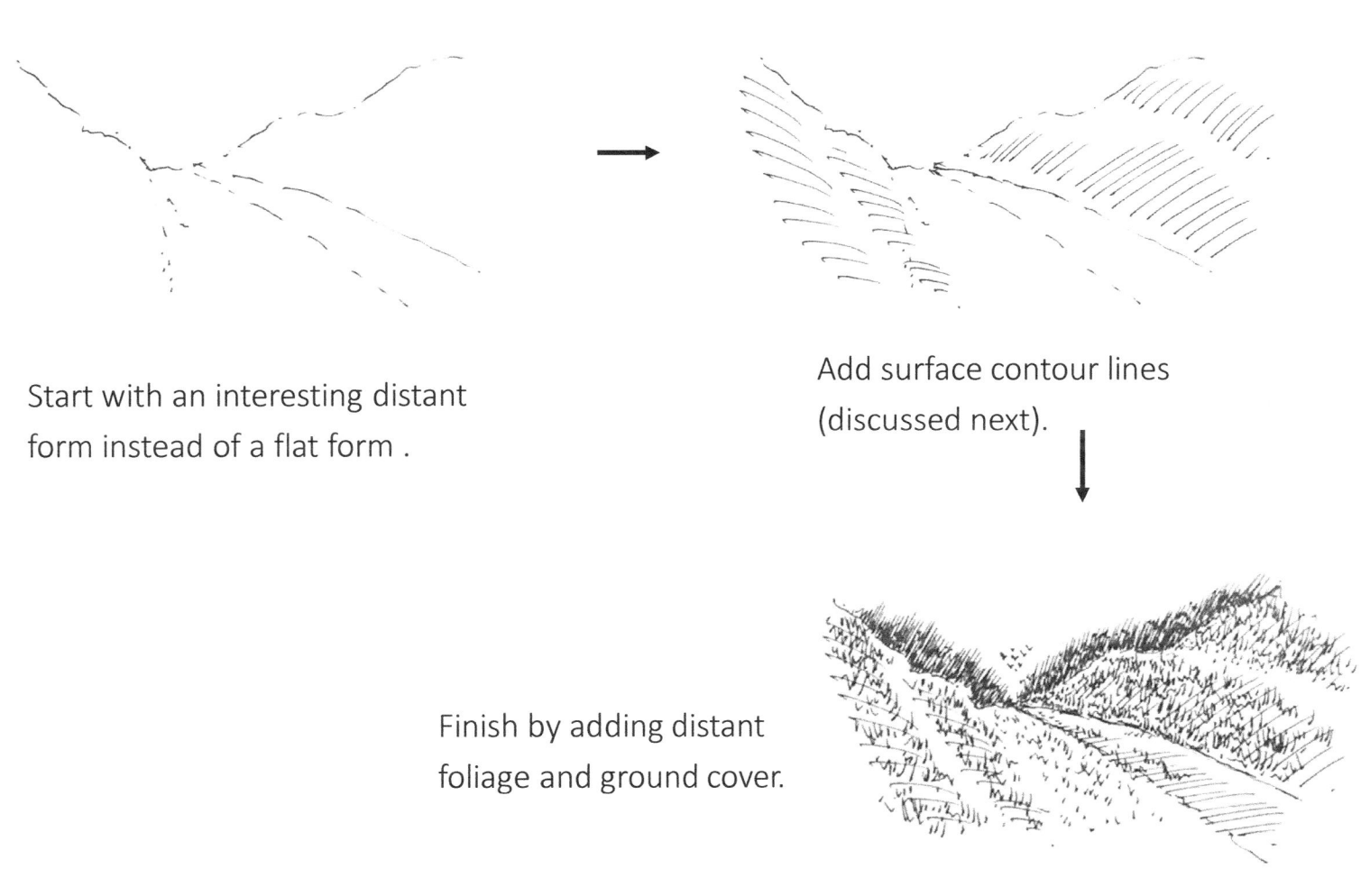

Start with an interesting distant form instead of a flat form .

Add surface contour lines (discussed next).

Finish by adding distant foliage and ground cover.

Drawing Surface Contours:

Contour of a surface can be suggested by using curved parallel lines as shown below. The curvature of the lines indicate the contour of the surface. Make then slightly tapered as shown below.

Such lines can be used to bring out the contour of the surface. ↓

A Simple Example

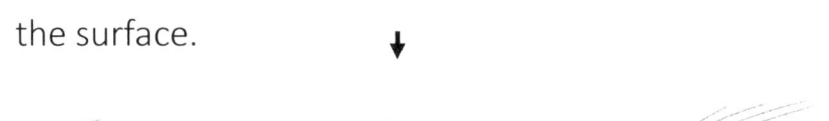

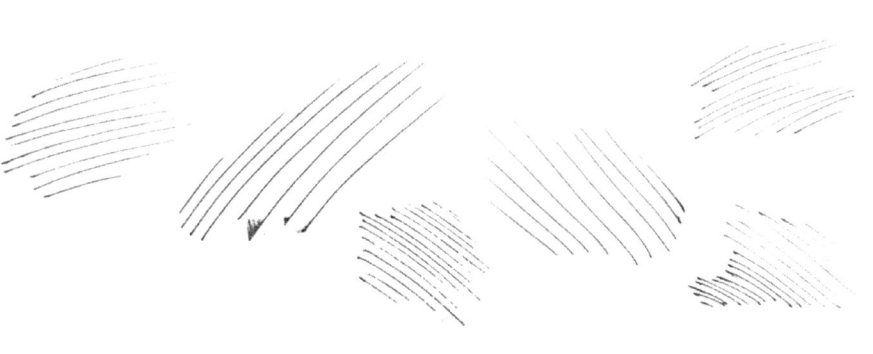

Start by drawing a distant form that indicates surface contours. Some kind of U shape works well.

↓

Finish by adding other elements. Such simple pleasing drawings are quick and always fun to do. ↓

Use contour lines to indicate surface contours. It should be in accordance with the form.

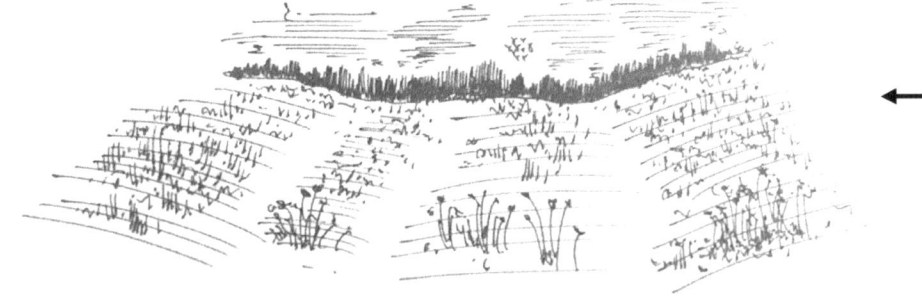

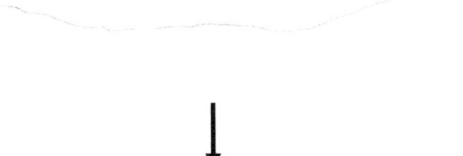

More Examples:

There is no limit to pleasing such landscapes that can be drawn with surface contours. Following are some more examples. Try one of your own.

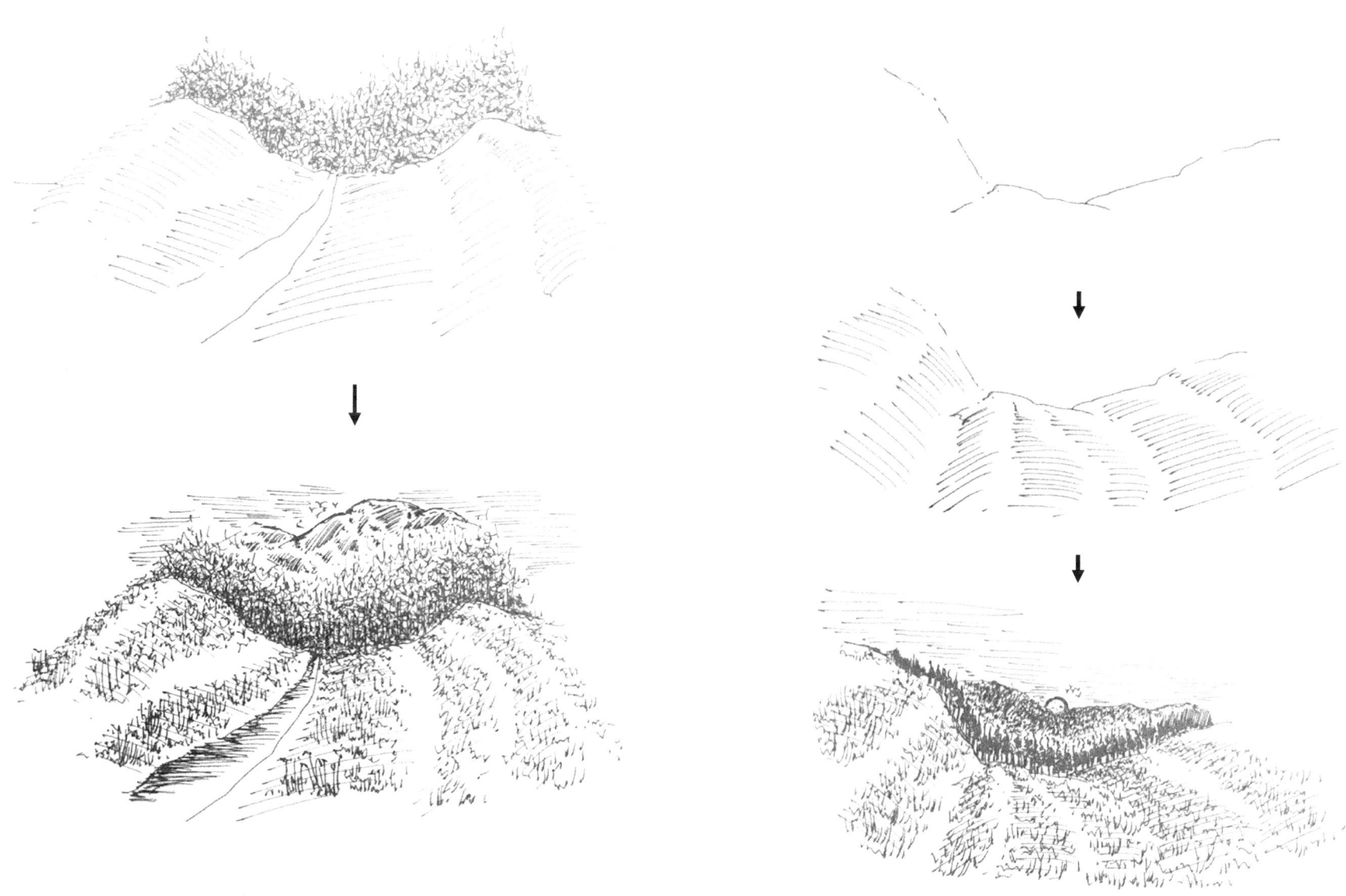

Some More Examples:

Some more examples to get you started. By combining different such elements, simple pleasing compositions like these can be easily drawn.

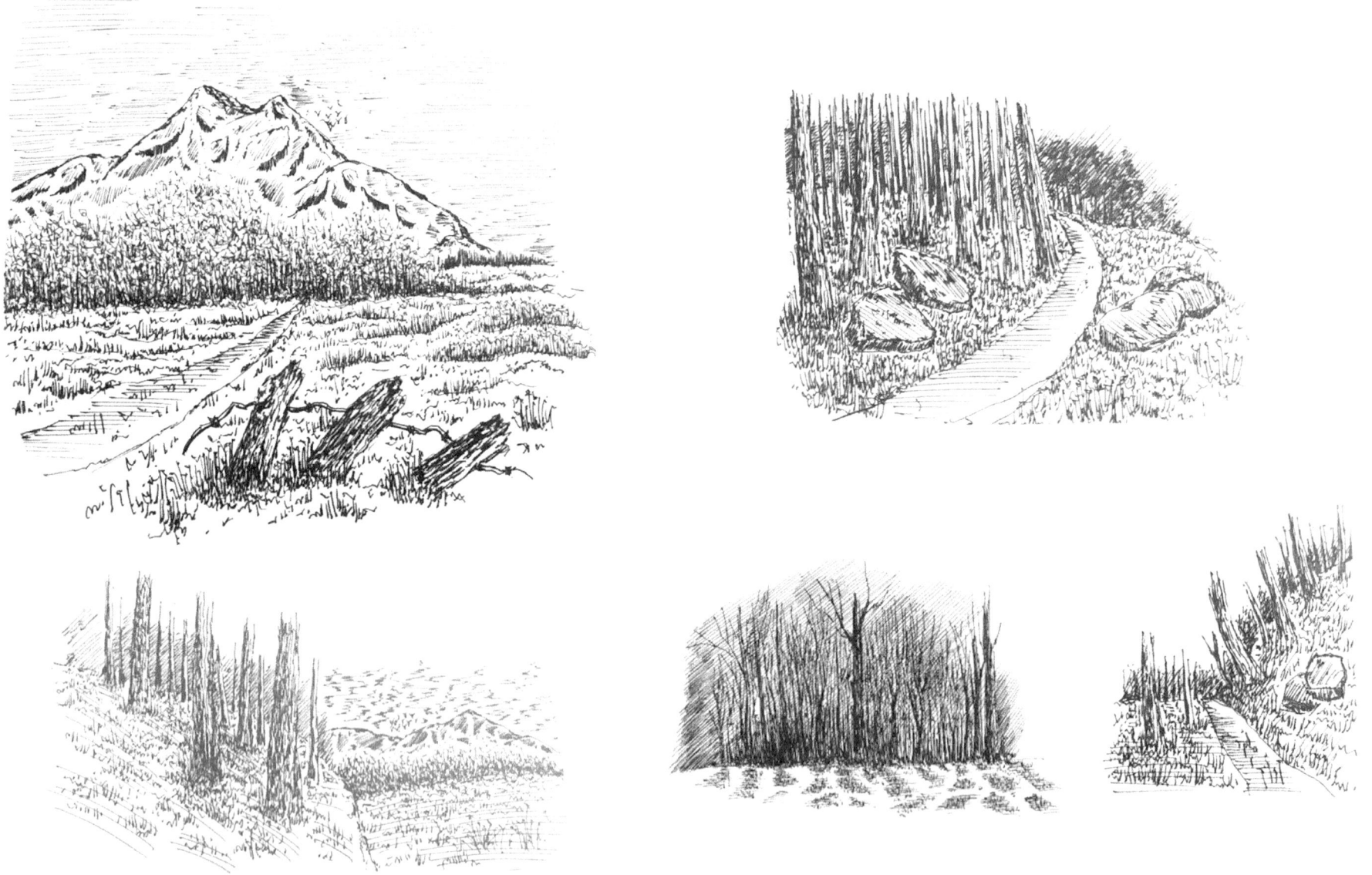

Drawing Ground Cover:

As we saw before, grass and ground cover is an important part of any wooded scene. Without some kind of ground cover, any wooded scene will look incomplete. Use following steps to draw grass at different distance from horizon.

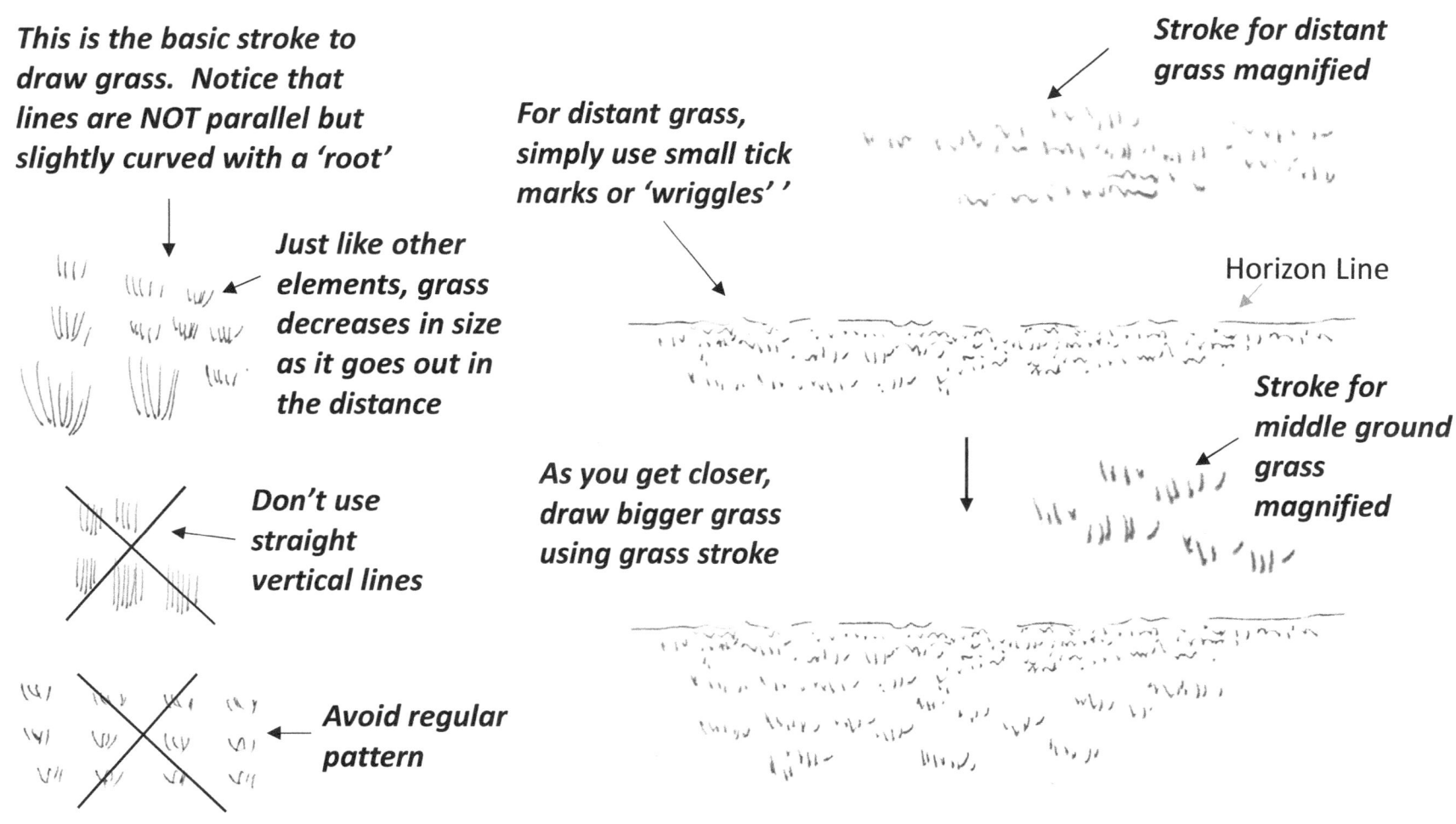

Drawing Ground Cover, Continued:

It is very important to observe perspective when drawing grass. This means drawing grass very small with just dots and ticks for distant grass and using bigger strokes for foreground grass as shown below.

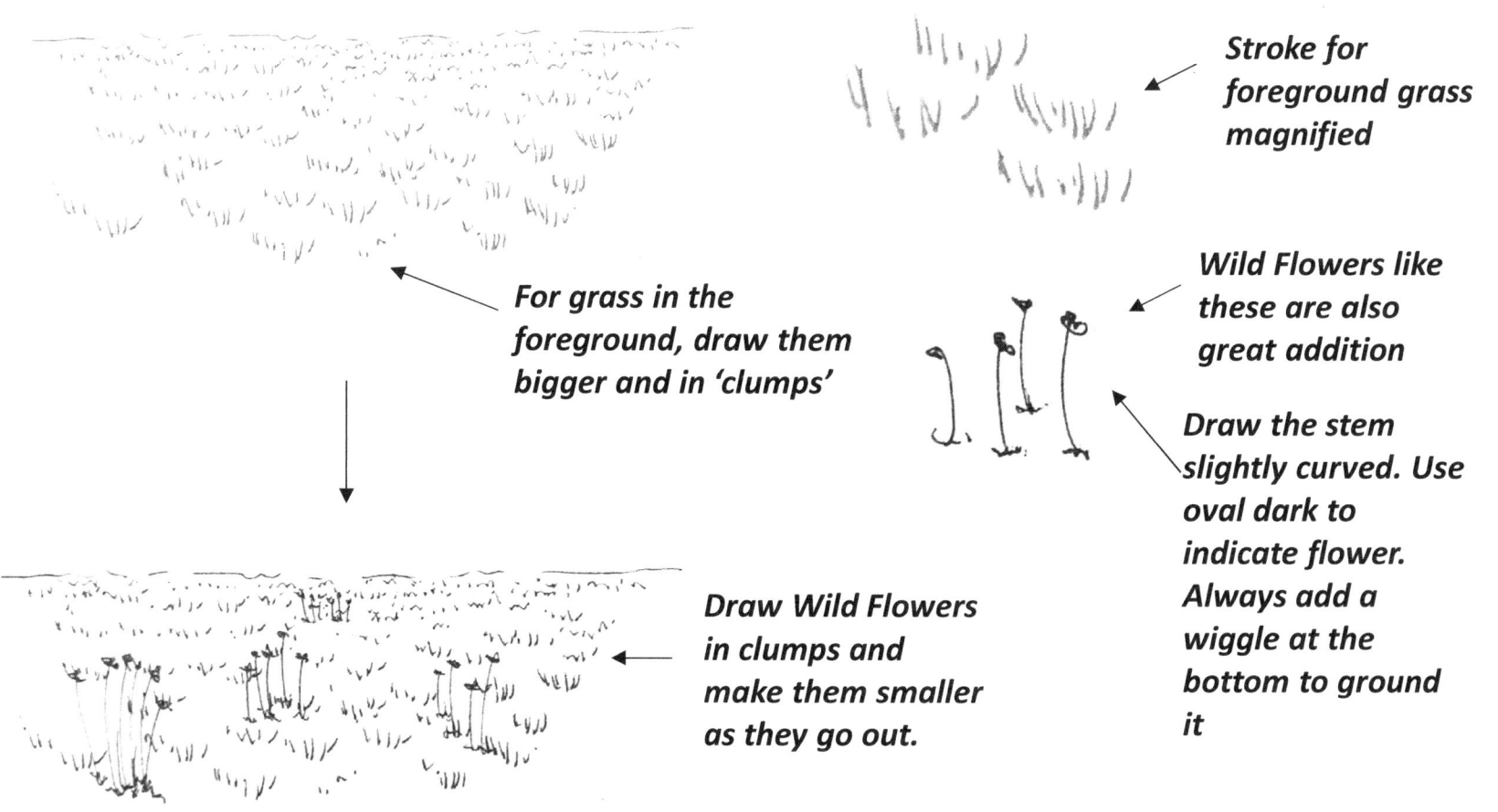

Stroke for foreground grass magnified

For grass in the foreground, draw them bigger and in 'clumps'

Wild Flowers like these are also great addition

Draw the stem slightly curved. Use oval dark to indicate flower. Always add a wiggle at the bottom to ground it

Draw Wild Flowers in clumps and make them smaller as they go out.

Relative intensity of ground cover :

Just some grass stroke is enough to give a feel of ground cover. Often explicit covering of all ground with grass is not needed. But more density of grass can be used to create different feel if needed.

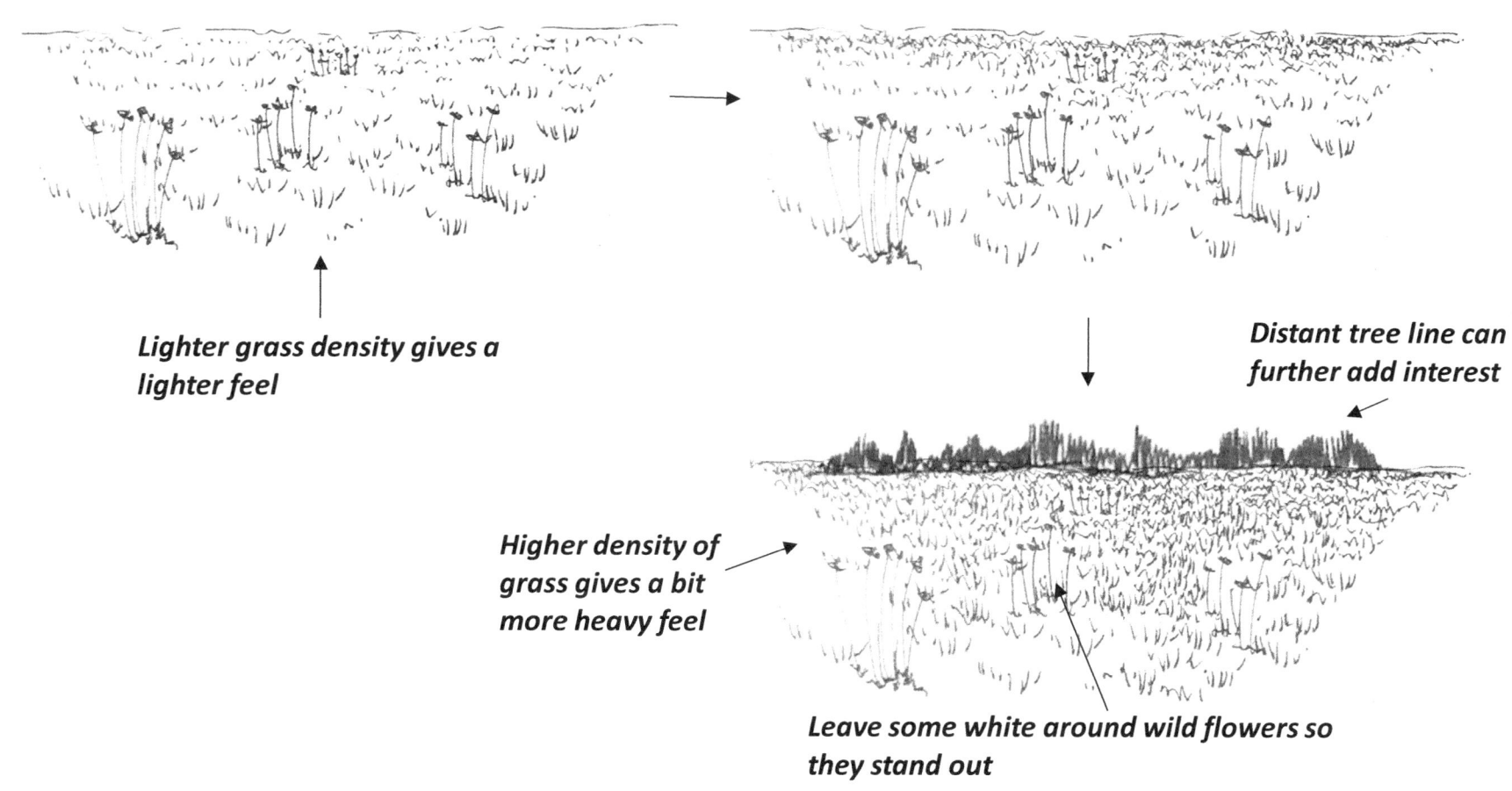

Lighter grass density gives a lighter feel

Higher density of grass gives a bit more heavy feel

Distant tree line can further add interest

Leave some white around wild flowers so they stand out

Activity: Drawing ground cover :

Draw grass and a distant element per earlier instructions below.

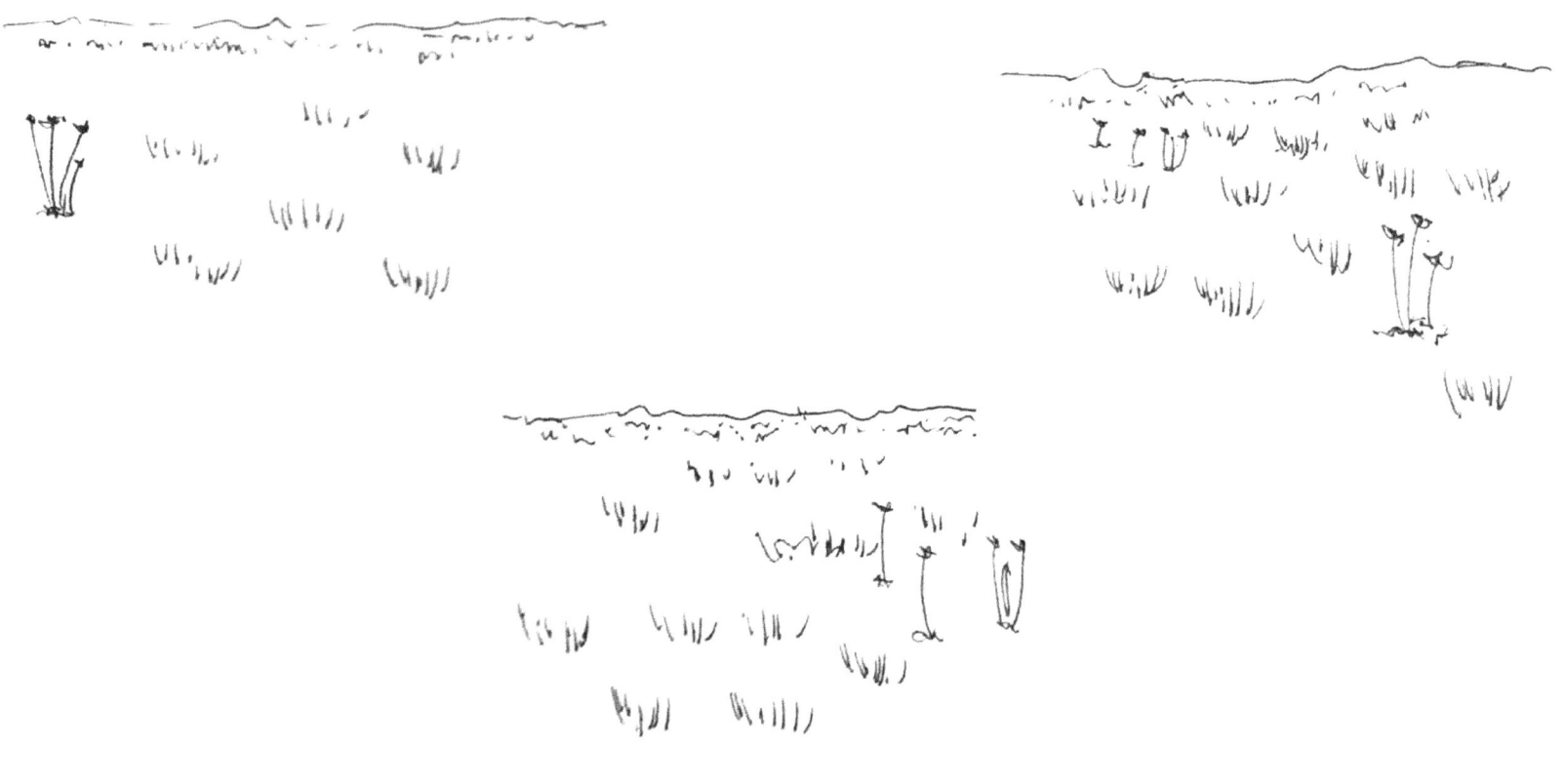

Final Thoughts:

This completes this workbook but hopefully this is just the beginning of your pen and ink drawing adventure. Drawing a wooded scene is very fun and can be easily done from imagination using simple techniques discussed in this workbook. Key is to start somewhere and then practice. Small daily practice is ideal. Carry a pocket sketch book and pen with you and in between your breaks trying putting simple quick drawings as illustrated in this workbook. Don't let initial frustration stop you in progressing on your creative journey. With practice you will steadily improve and discover that drawing is not just for 'artists' but is something that can be part of all of us in exploring and expressing our creative sides with a simple medium like a pen and paper.

Don't be afraid to explore with pen. Let your hands express freely and without reservation. If you feel like making a scramble of lines, do so. A big part of drawing with pen and ink is letting go of your inhibitions about use of pen and specifically putting a 'wrong' line. With simple strokes and techniques presented in this and other workbooks in the series, I am confidant that you have the information you need to get started on this wonderful journey.

You can visit my website for completely free tutorials and use other workbooks I have created to learn how to draw other elements of nature, like trunks, stones etc. with pen and ink and create more interesting landscapes.

www.pendrawings.me/workbooks

Any comments, suggestions and feedback on improving contents of this workbook are most welcome. For more information on drawing landscapes with pen and ink, to learn more about my works and to reach me, please visit my website.

www.pendrawings.me/getstarted

Happy drawing,

Rahul Jain

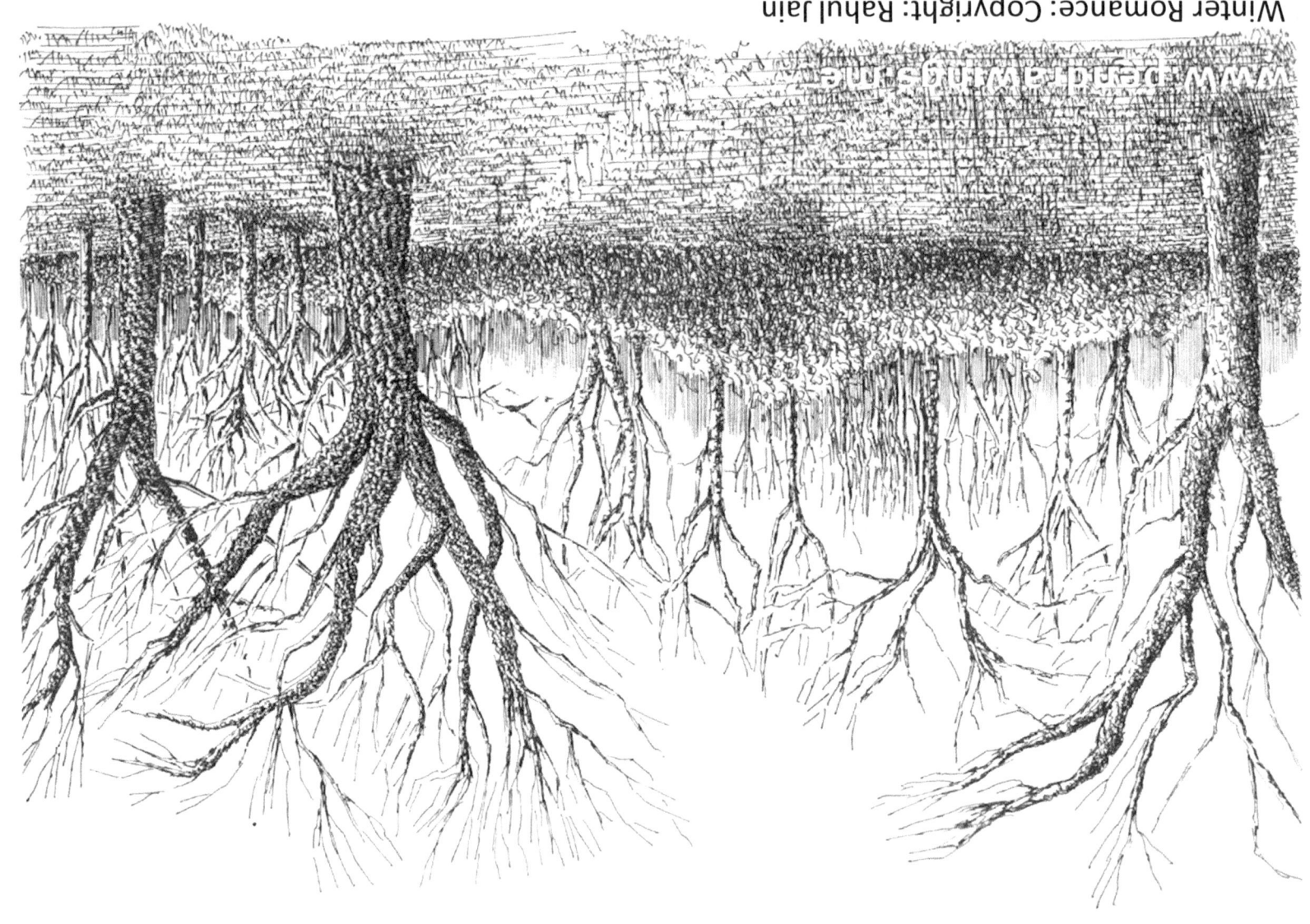

Winter Romance: Copyright: Rahul Jain

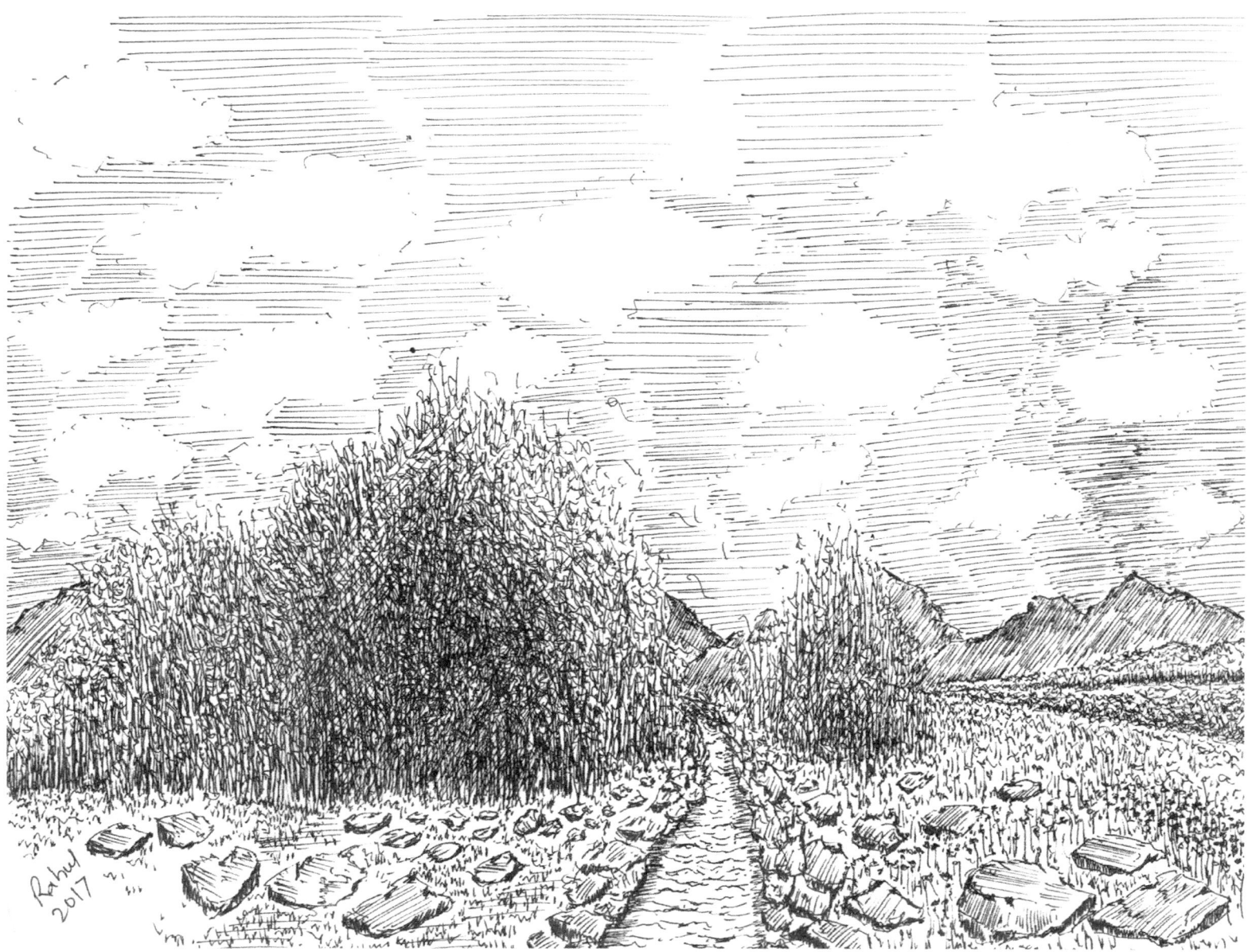

Gently Down the Stream: Copyright: Rahul Jain

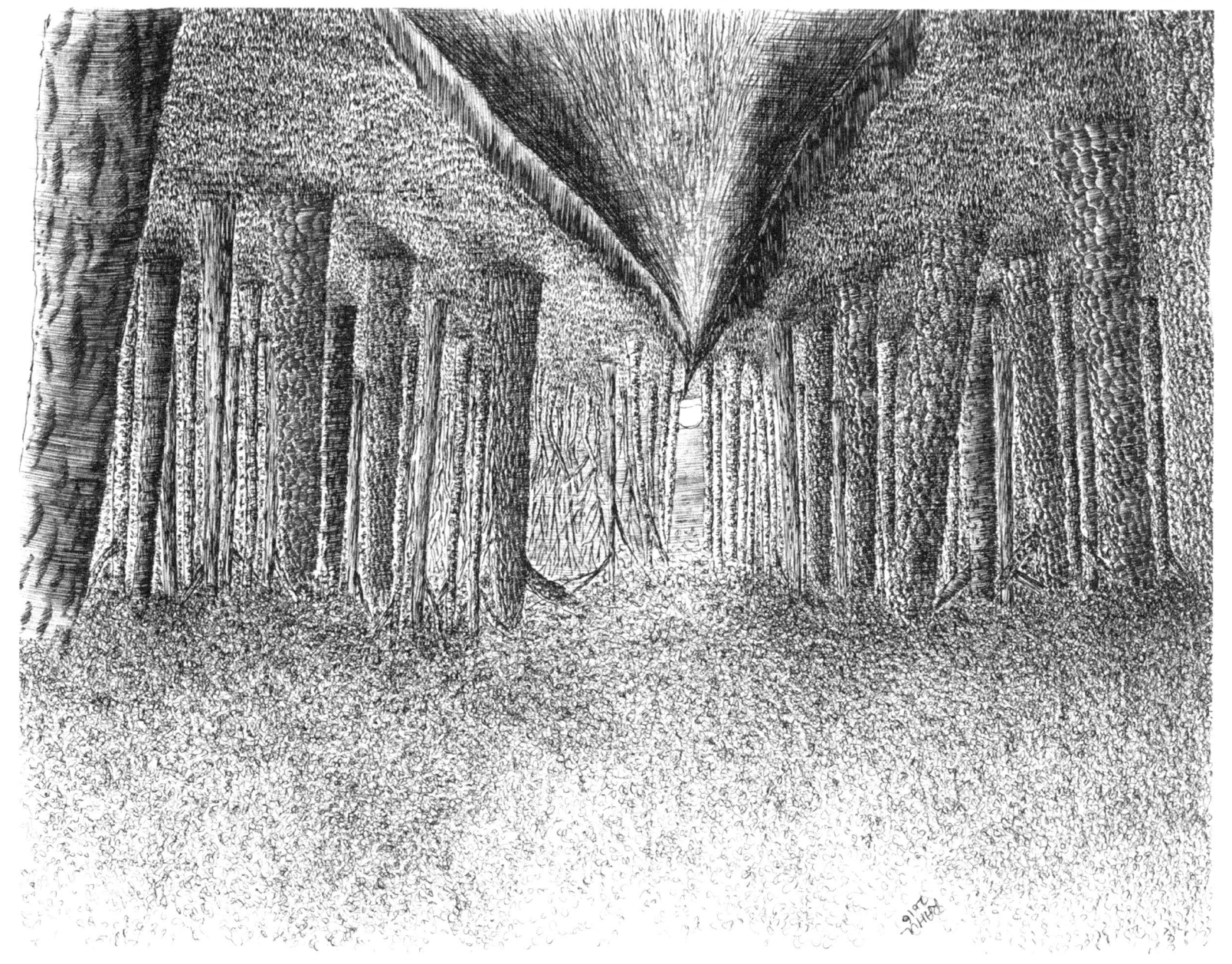

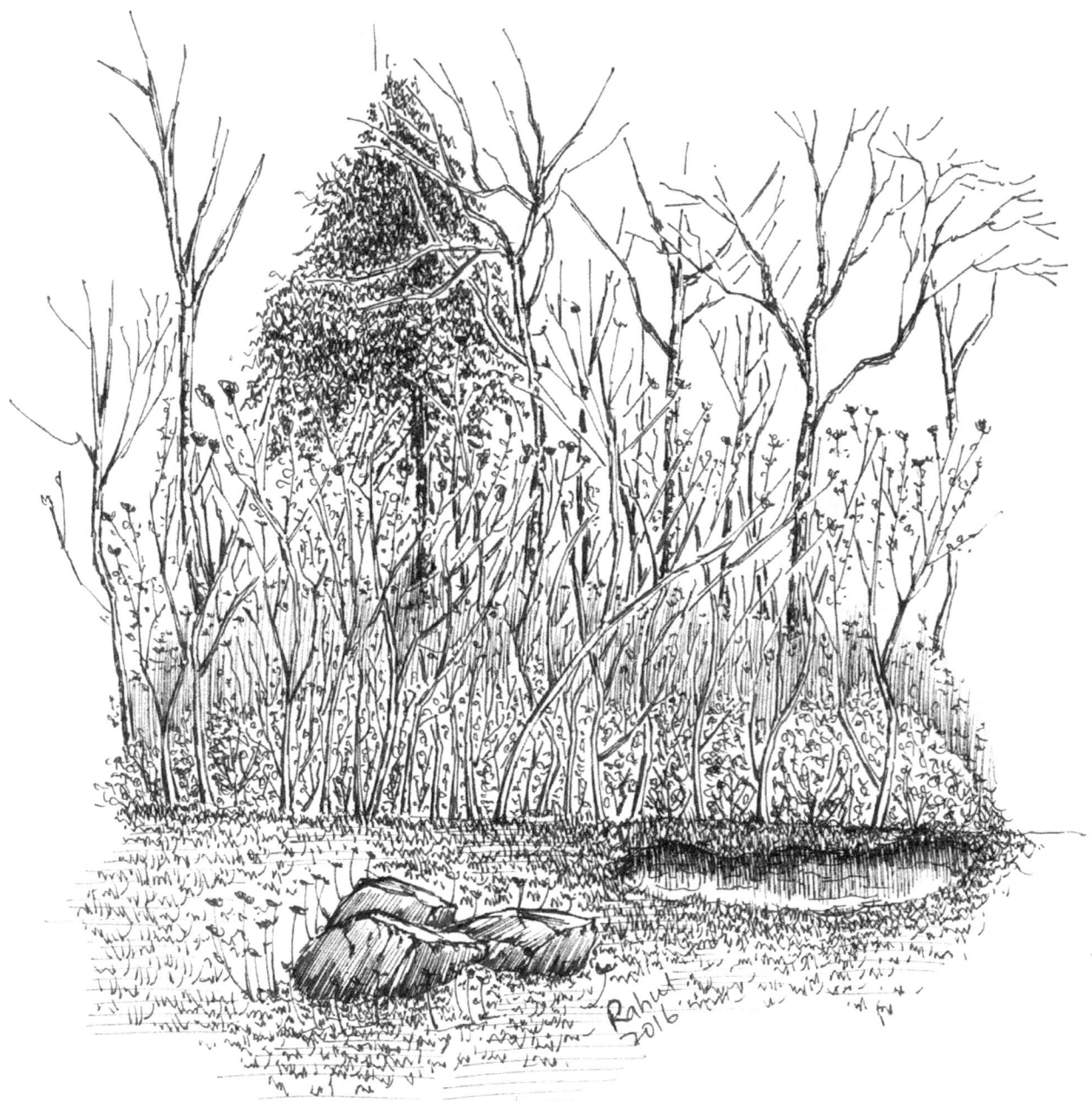

Winter Romance 2: Copyright: Rahul Jain

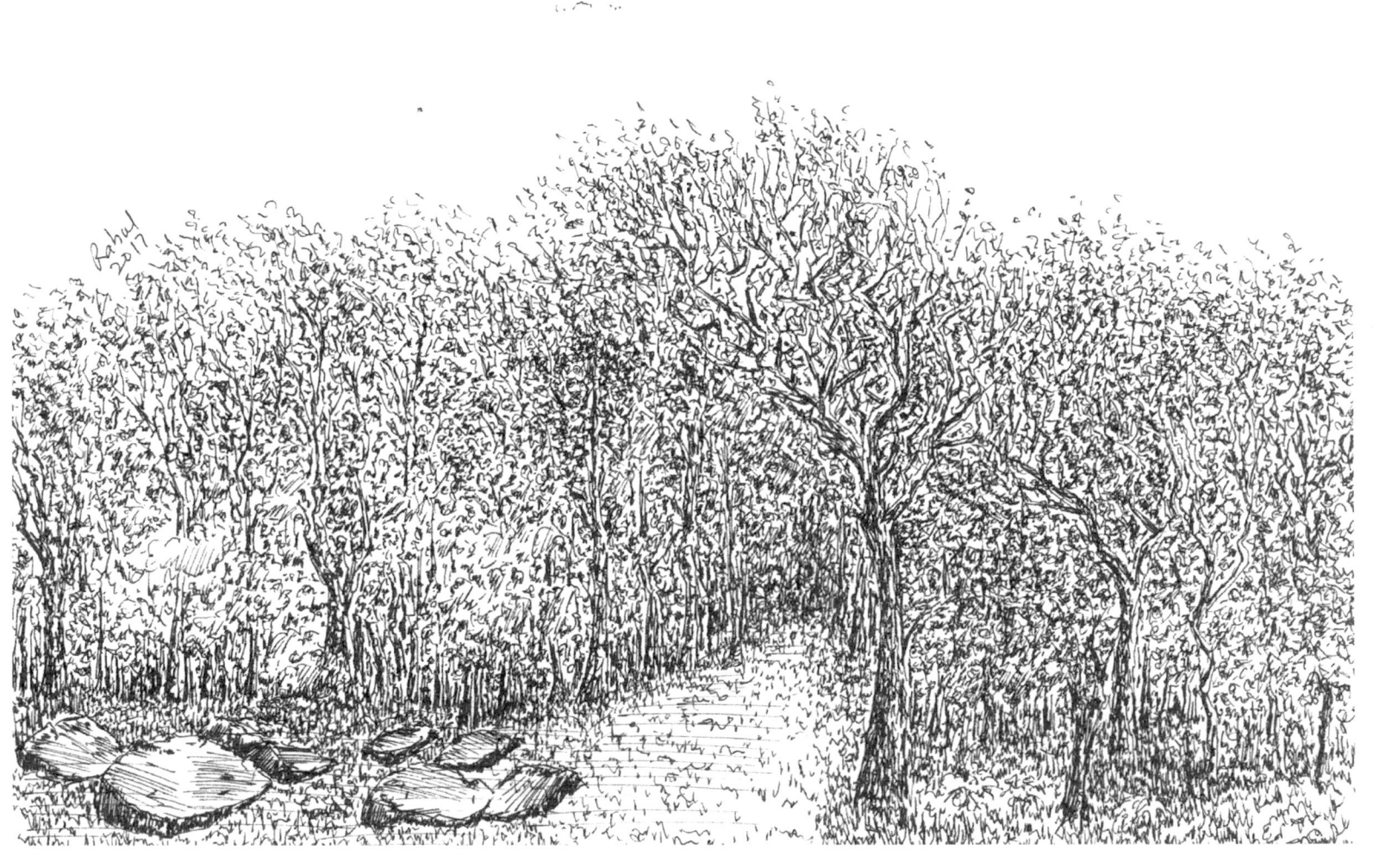

Where the Path May Lead: Copyright: Rahul Jain

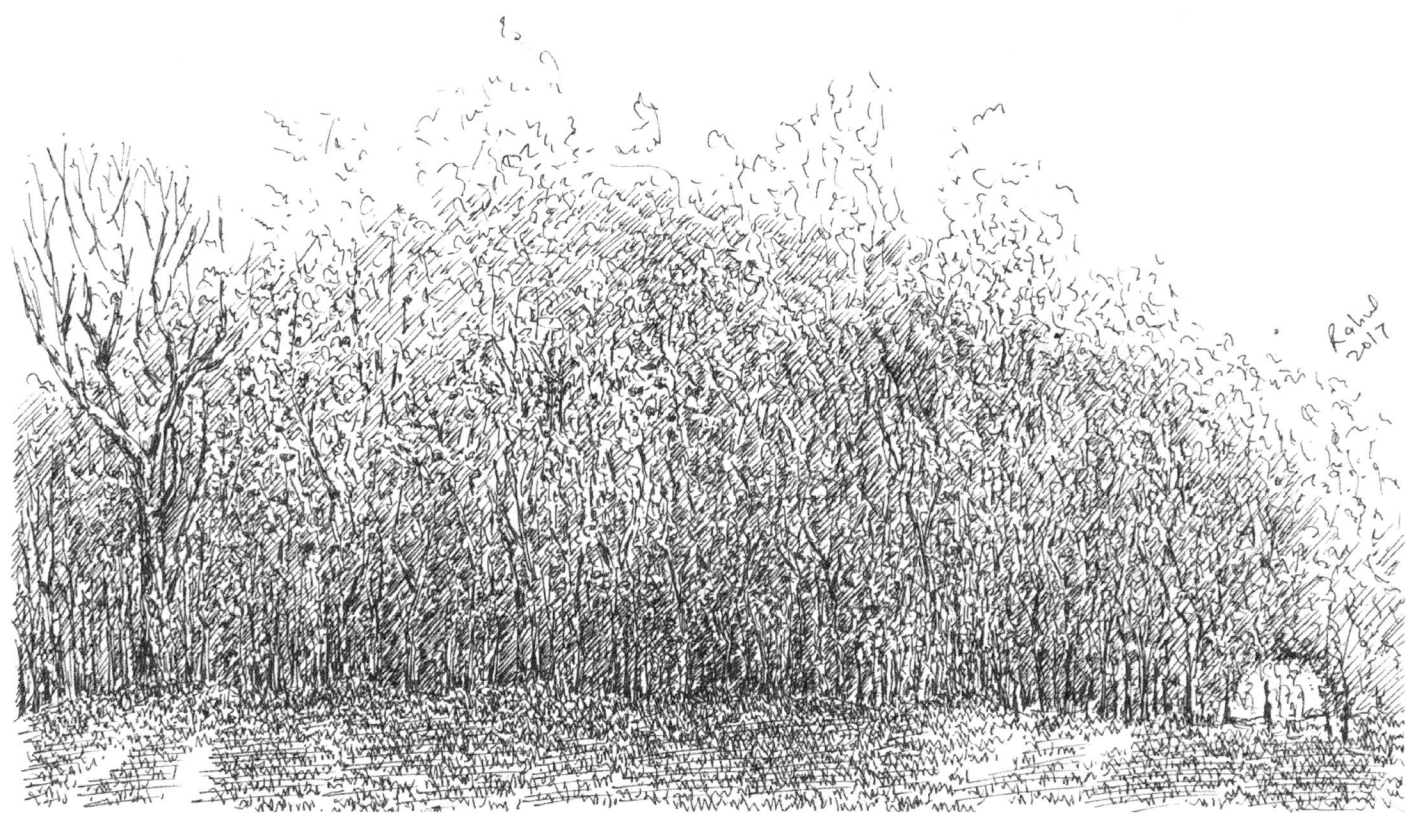

Call of Nature: Copyright: Rahul Jain

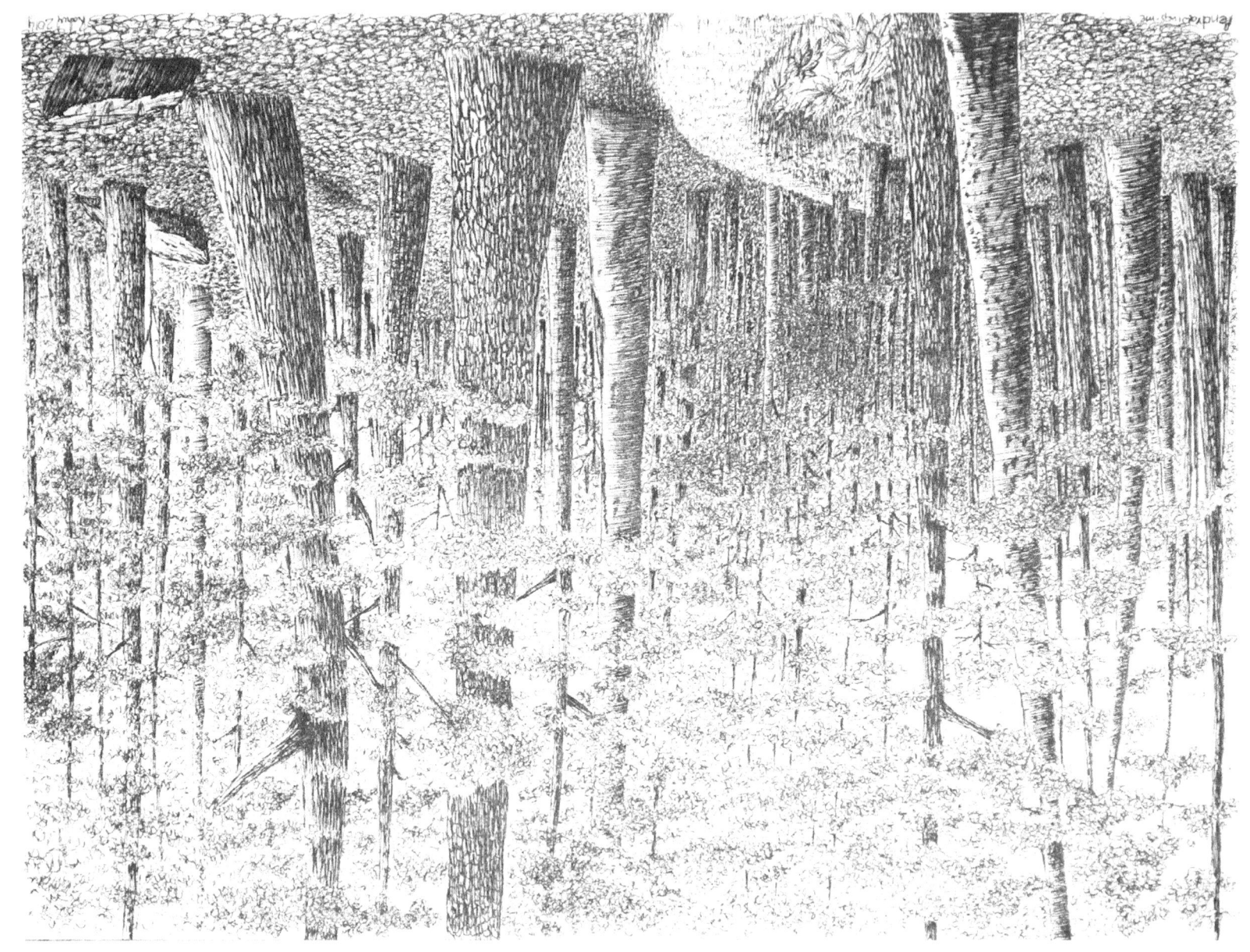

A Walk in the Woods: Copyright: Rahul Jain

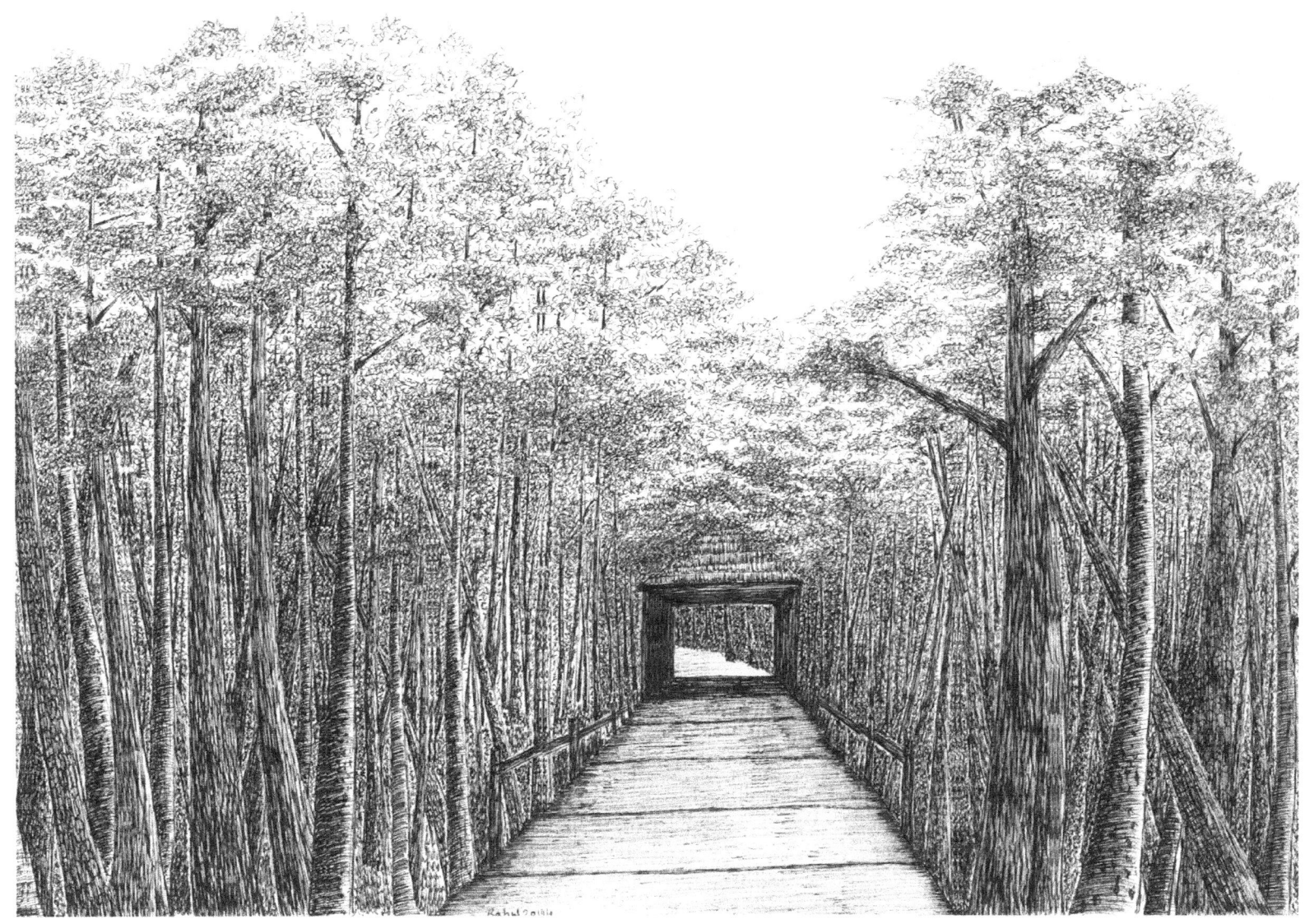

Enchanted Journey: Copyright: Rahul Jain

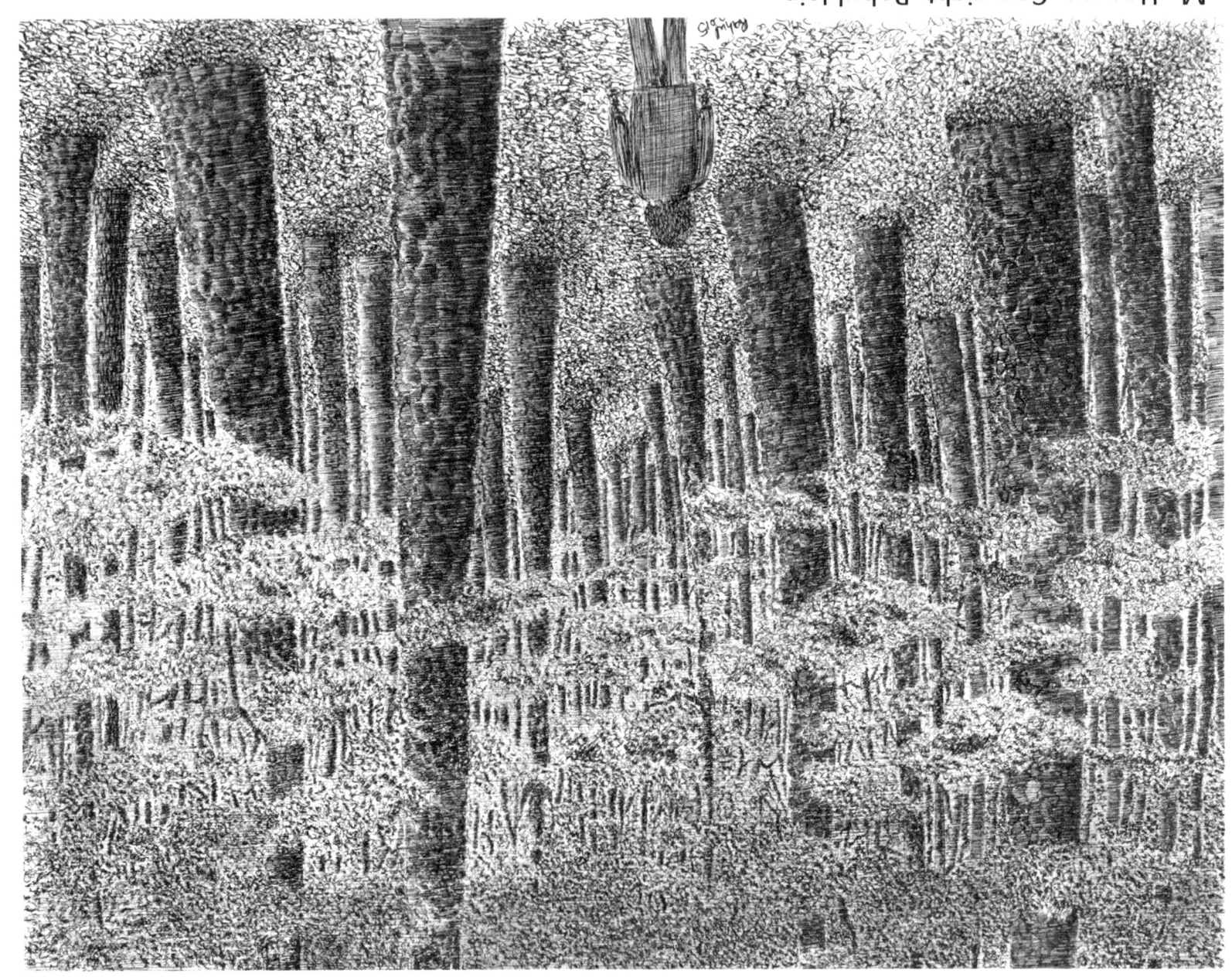